# Politics, Poverty, and Microfinance

# GLOBALIZATION AND ITS COSTS

## Series Editor:
## Dhirendra Vajpeyi, University of Northern Iowa

The last two decades of the 20th century witnessed drastic political and economic changes. As the sole superpower in world affairs, the U.S. has used its economic and military power to shape the rest of the world in its own image. Hence the need to develop a balanced, just, and holistic approach not only to meet the narrow trade and finance interests of developed democracies but also to encompass other crucial global concerns such as environmental degradation, human rights, immigration, private and public governance, poverty, income inequality, and political instability—issues and challenges directly or indirectly connected to human security. Though globalization has elevated hundreds of millions of people around the world from dire poverty, it has posed new challenges to humanity. *Globalization and Its Costs* will include analytical and empirical work from scholars in a comparative context. Topics should be of current interest, interdisciplinary and policy-oriented, and broadly related to human security and sustainable development paradigms.

### Advisory Board

Constantine Danopoulos, San Jose State University
Ramkumar Mishra, Osmania University
Hellmut Woolman, Humboldt University

### Books in Series

*Corporate Social Responsibility and Sustainable Development in Emerging Economies*, Edited by Dhirendra Vajpeyi and Roopinder Oberoi

*Politics, Poverty, and Microfinance: How Governments Get in the Way of Helping the Poor*, By Brian Warby

# Politics, Poverty, and Microfinance

## How Governments Get in the Way of Helping the Poor

Brian Warby

LEXINGTON BOOKS
*Lanham • Boulder • New York • London*

Published by Lexington Books
An imprint of The Rowman & Littlefield Publishing Group, Inc.
4501 Forbes Boulevard, Suite 200, Lanham, Maryland 20706
www.rowman.com

Unit A, Whitacre Mews, 26-34 Stannary Street, London SE11 4AB, United Kingdom

British Library Cataloguing in Publication Information Available

**Library of Congress Cataloging-in-Publication Data**

Names: Warby, Brian, author.
Title: Politics, poverty, and microfinance : how governments get in the way of helping the poor / Brian Warby.
Description: Lanham : Lexington Books, [2016] | Series: Globalization and its costs | Includes bibliographical references and index.
Identifiers: LCCN 2015036065| ISBN 9781498517522 (cloth : alk. paper) | ISBN 9781498517546 (pbk. : alk. paper) | ISBN 9781498517539 (electronic)
Subjects: LCSH: Microfinance—Political aspects. | Poor—Government policy—Developing countries. | Poverty—Government policy—Developing countries. | Economic development—Developing countries.
Classification: LCC HG178.3 .W37 2016 | DDC 362.5/561—dc23 LC record available at http://lccn.loc.gov/2015036065

♾TM The paper used in this publication meets the minimum requirements of American National Standard for Information Sciences—Permanence of Paper for Printed Library Materials, ANSI/NISO Z39.48-1992.

Printed in the United States of America

I dedicate this book to my wife, Candice Warby,
my mother, Denice Blake, and
my late father, Brent Warby,
all of whom have supported and
loved me unconditionally.

# Contents

# Figures and Tables

## FIGURES

## TABLES

# Acronyms

| | |
|---|---|
| APR | Annualized Percentage Rate |
| CCT | Conditional Cash Transfer |
| CGAP | Consultative Group to Assist the Poor |
| EIU | Economist Intelligence Unit |
| FDI | Foreign Direct Investment |
| GDP | Gross Domestic Product |
| IADB | Inter-American Development Bank |
| IGO | Inter-Governmental Organization |
| IMF | International Monetary Fund |
| ISI | Import-Substitution Industrialization |
| MFI | Microfinance Institution |
| MIV | Microfinance Investment Vehicle |
| MIX | Microfinance Information Exchange |
| NGO | Non-Governmental Organization |
| OECD | Organization for Economic Cooperation and Development |
| UN | United Nations |

# Preface

My research on microfinance spawned from an interest in global poverty. Not long after graduating from high school I had the opportunity to spend a considerable amount of time living in Brazil, not as a tourist but as part of the community. During that time, I saw, and experienced to a limited degree, the living conditions that were common among the poorer classes of Brazilians. At the time I observed their conditions passively. However, upon returning to the United States, I realized how differently my middle-class family lived from most of my Brazilian friends. I tried to reconcile the luxuries middle-class Americans take for granted with the basic needs for which billions of people must constantly struggle. I could not see that my new friends worked less or were any less intelligent than middle-class Americans, but their incomes were only a fraction of the average American's income. I wanted to know why, and whether anything could be done about it.

When I began learning about microfinance, I read the glowing reports from the Grameen Bank and other NGOs and IGOs around the world. It seemed like a solution that could help eradicate global poverty. The logic of providing capital to people who were capital poor appealed to my western, liberal economic training. It seemed like a plausible and sustainable solution to poverty. However, the more I read about microfinance the more I questioned its impact and effectiveness. Skeptics of microfinance had some convincing data to show that microfinance might not be as impactful as early proponents had suggested.

The research presented in this book is part of an international effort to address global poverty. Millions of people face the constant threat of death due to their impoverished conditions. Billions more live in deprivation. As a global society, this is something we should be concerned about and try to resolve for the benefit of humanity. Our current interventions have only limited impact. The global community is making steady, if slow, progress on health-related interventions, and I applaud their success, but in order to sustainably improve the living conditions of the poor, we have to increase their incomes. On that front, we have seen meager progress outside of a handful of developing countries. The problem is that we still do not know how to implement practical, effective policies that benefit the entire cross-section of a society and not just the elites.

I approach this project as a researcher looking for solutions to poverty. Only by understanding how our current approaches to poverty alleviation work, and how effective they are, can we effectively address a major global problem. The results of my analyses are presented in a way that offers answers to one of the big questions about microfinance effectiveness—what role governments play. The results offer useful conclusions for policy makers, practitioners and social activists alike. It is my hope that this research will contribute to the global effort to combat poverty.

## ACKNOWLEDGMENTS

This book is the result of several years of research. During that time, many people have helped me in a variety of ways. I first wish to thank those who have provided emotional and moral support along the way. My wife, Candice, has never wavered in supporting me in my academic and professional endeavors. She has always been willing to listen while I talk through my ideas and as I work through the challenges and puzzles that inevitably arise with any research project. Her words of encouragement often strengthened my resolve to push forward on the project. I must also express my deep gratitude to my mother, Denice Blake. She has always loved, supported and encouraged me as only a mother can. Finally, I am grateful to my late father, Brent Warby, whose example of persistence and hard work I have tried to follow.

I would also like to thank Lee Walker and Jerel Rosati for their feedback and suggestions during the early stages of this project. Their advice helped me think about how to frame the research and helped me refine my analyses. I must include the editor of this series, Dhirendra Vajpeyi, as well. He has mentored me through the publication process and helped me turn a research agenda into a book. His advice and assistance have been invaluable.

Many other people have also helped shape my ideas or offered support along the way. I am indebted to Gerald McDermott for his comments on this project; to Joshua Ault who helped me establish professional contacts; and to Valerie Kindt at ACCION and Mark Wenner at the Inter-American Development Bank for speaking with me and offering their perspectives on microfinance. I want to profusely thank Brenda Bass, dean of the College of Social and Behavioral Sciences at the University of Northern Iowa, and Donna Hoffman, head of the Department of Political Science at the University of Northern Iowa, who have offered professional support for the project.

# Chapter One

# Introduction

Microfinance is a topic about which there are many debates regarding its effectiveness, purpose, and ideal and legitimate forms. While there are many important questions that yet remain unanswered, one of the key questions is whether microfinance actually helps the people it is said to help—those who live below or near poverty levels. The debate is illustrated by the following two stories.

The first story was originally told by Muhammad Yunus, founder of the Grameen Bank and recipient of the Nobel Peace Prize for his work on poverty alleviation.

> Murshida was born to a poor family and married an unskilled factory worker when she was 15 years old. Her husband had a gambling problem and was physically abusive. His gambling got so bad that he sold the roof off of their humble house to pay his debts. When Murshida confronted him about his neglecting her and their three children he went into a rage, beat her and divorced her on the spot. Murshida took her children to her brother's house where she found some work spinning. When the Grameen Bank came to her village she persistently sought out a small loan.
>
> At first Murshida borrowed 1,000 taka [about $30] to purchase a goat and she paid off the loan in six months with the profits from selling the milk. She was left with a goat, a kid, and no debt. Encouraged, she borrowed 2,000 taka, bought raw cotton and a spinning wheel, and began manufacturing lady's scarves, which she sells for 50–100 taka each. She also employs up to twenty-five other women from her village during peak season. She also used a Grameen Bank housing loan to build a house on an acre of farmland and set up her brothers in business trading saris and raw cotton (Roodman 2012).[1]

The next story was documented in a film by Tom Heinemann called *The Micro Debt*:

> Razia, a woman living in a small village in the northern part of Bangladesh, had a relatively comfortable life style, with her own house, cows, and jewelry. She took a loan from Grameen Bank to pay for her daughter's education, but found herself unable to repay the loan.
>
> "I had no money to pay the installments. So I decided to sell the house. These [microfinance] organizations never stop. They really pressed me. They come and stay until they get their money. They press us to sell our belongings. So I sold the house to pay the debt." After selling the house her family built, she lamented, "I have nothing left to sell, except the kitchen pots" (Roodman 2012).

In reading these two very different stories about how microfinance affected people's lives, one cannot help but question why the two outcomes were so dramatically different. Of course, these are complex processes and there are a variety of contributing factors. Many scholars have studied microfinance in order to better understand what those factors are and how the processes work. The two stories above show that microfinance can be a powerful tool, either for good, helping to improve the quality of life of customers, or for harm, stripping from the near poor their thin cushion against poverty and leaving them entirely destitute. If microfinance generally follows the pattern displayed in the first story, wide and extensive implementation should help improve the quality of life for the poor all over the world. On the other hand, if it tends to follow the pattern in the second story, global implementation could be disastrous. So, which is it? This has been one of the main debates, though certainly not the only debate, about microfinance over the last fifteen years or so. The answer is that it might be both, depending on the conditions in which microfinance is operating.

The key is to figure out when and where microfinance might work and might not work. If we can do this, we might be able to re-create Murshida's story *en masse* and avoid replicating Razia's story. Unfortunately, this is not an easy task. The discussion within microfinance circles, and development activists more broadly, has failed to pick up on some of the nuances. The discussion is generally stuck in arguing over whether microfinance works or not, with one side asserting that it helps alleviate poverty and the other side, at first skeptical, then growing bolder in its assertion that it has no beneficial impact on the poor. Much of the discussion is focused on a single dimension when, in reality, there are many dimensions that should be considered.

The multi-dimensionality of microfinance likely comes as no surprise to the reader since human nature, culture, markets and political systems are all quite complex. It seems almost comical to try and hold a discussion on something like poverty alleviation that cuts across the entire globe, while addressing only a single dimension. In fact, many of the experts who are engaged in this single-dimensional debate implicitly acknowledge the multi-dimensionality of the problem when they talk about the factors that might influence a microfinance customer or a microfinance lender to pursue a particular course of action. We also see it in their regressions as they control for a host of intervening factors. But most fail to discuss how these nuances may change their answers under different conditions. To be fair, adding multiple dimensions to the question makes it more difficult to understand and philanthropists and social investors prefer simple, intuitive, and empirically verifiable answers when they ask whether an intervention works. This book focuses on just one additional dimension—government—and how it affects microfinance's impact on the lives of the poor.

## WHY STUDY MICROFINANCE?

In 2000, the United Nations (UN) held the Millennium Summit, which adopted the UN Millennium Declaration. The declaration represents a commitment to improve the quality of life of people in the developing world. The declaration and subsequent negotiations and summits outlined a number of specific, verifiable goals that the global community could work towards in order to combat the world's number one killer and perpetuator of human misery—poverty. The community came up with eight Millennium Development Goals (MDGs), which ranged from eradicating extreme poverty and hunger, to promoting gender equality and creating a global partnership for development. In 2010, representatives from states from around the world met again to work on the MDGs and pledged more than $40 billion in resources to help achieve the desired outcomes. Unfortunately, in 2015, the deadline year for the goals, we can only claim partial success, but that has not deterred development efforts.[2] The global community continues to strive to eliminate poverty and hunger. One of the greatest obstacles in this struggle, however, is the lack of consensus on how to reduce poverty and help the poorest countries develop.

A survey of popular titles by economists over the last decade tells the story, from Paul Collier's *The Bottom Billion: Why the Poorest Countries Are Failing and What Can Be Done About It* (2007), to Jeffrey Sachs's *The End of Poverty: Economic Possibilities for Our Time* (2005), or William Easterly's titles *The Elusive Quest for Growth: Economists' Adventures and Misadventures in the Tropics* (2001) and *The White Man's Burden: Why the West's Efforts to Aid the Rest Have Done So Much Ill and So Little Good* (2006). There are a number of posited solutions, of course, which tend to drive the debate on. Some scholars, like Sachs, argue that digging wells, building dams and highways, donating computers to schools and all of the other projects typically associated with development are necessary to help the developing countries make their way on to the global playing field as viable competitors. On the other side are economists like William Easterly, who does not hold such a rosy view of the world. He ridicules traditional development aid as "utopian blueprints" that sound revolutionary but never fully accomplish what they set out to do (Easterly 2006). He argues instead that development must proceed in a more natural, even biological process, that can be fed a healthy diet of laissez-faire policies and political stability, but which follows a unique path to maturity because no two countries face the same constraints on their political systems, societies or economies. Finally, foreign aid is hailed in some circles as the way forward, as proposed in *Aid That Works: Successful Development in Fragile States* (Manor 2007), but in other circles it is questioned or even dismissed as ineffective or as *The Aid Trap* (Hubbard and Duggan 2009).

Clearly, the economic development literature is far from achieving consensus on how to help poor countries grow, or how to help poor people in those countries achieve higher standards of living. While a great deal of research has examined the intricacies of foreign aid, foreign direct investment (FDI), loan forgiveness, and membership in organizations such as the International Monetary Fund (IMF), much less research has examined microfinance and its effectiveness. This may be in part because microfinance, at the scale we see today, is a relatively new phenomenon (Roodman 2012). Although it has only recently received as much attention as other approaches to economic growth and poverty alleviation, it is, in many ways, a unique approach.

Microfinance is especially interesting because it is an economic development technique that relies far less on the state than most others. Foreign aid, for example, is a government-to-government intervention, which means it is inherently politicized (Hubbard and Duggan 2009). When renowned political scientist Hans Morgenthau wrote about foreign aid in 1962 he identified six different categories of foreign aid and concluded that only one of those categories, disaster relief aid, might be politically neutral (Morgenthau 1962). Unfortunately, even disaster relief aid is often politicized. When typhoon Haiyan struck the Philippines in early November 2013, many villages were devastated, more than six thousand people were killed and millions were displaced. Not surprisingly, the global community responded with disaster relief aid. Rich countries and poor countries alike offered what they could to help the Philippine government address both the immediate humanitarian needs and the long-term cleanup and rebuilding effort. China, however, the second largest economy in the world, offered a paltry $100,000. The offer was perceived by much of the global community as an insult because China and the Philippines had been disputing control over a group of islands in the South China Sea (Einhorn 2013).[3]

Foreign aid is subject to the whims of the donor government and the capacity and corruption of the recipient government. Foreign aid flows tend to dry up during recessions, which is precisely when recipient governments most need the help (Hubbard and Duggan 2009). Donors often tie aid to political favors or policies that leave them in a bad position (Chang 2012). Recipients often suffer from corrupt officials who pilfer portions of the aid, and from a lack of capacity to use aid effectively (Acemoglu and Robinson 2012). When some leaders receive aid, they might simply substitute it for government spending in a particular area, such as education, thus allowing the government to spend its own funds elsewhere (Easterly 2006).

Similarly, FDI is highly subject to the whims and policies of the recipient state. A recipient state might decide to appropriate investments within its borders. It might also seek bribes or engage in other rent-seeking behavior in regard to investors (Bueno de Mesquita and Smith 2011). It might also simply impose high taxes in one form or another on FDI in order to extract some benefit (Busse and Hefeker 2007; Daude and Stein 2007; Kolstad and Villanger 2008). For example, many FDI projects failed in Vietnam during the early reform period, 1988–1998. Failure may have been associated with the government's lingering preferences for some industries over others, with the lack of communication and transportation between the north and south of the country and weak government support for foreign investment (Kokko, Kotoglou, and Krohwinkel-Karlsson 2003).

The relationship between microfinance and the state, however, is far more tenuous. The government might be able to affect the microfinance industry through regulation, but that is often the extent of its control over this market. Much of the activity in microfinance occurs at the individual level. Individuals are engaging in financial relationships with companies or organizations and could potentially never interact directly with the government in any form. In fact, microfinance is really a formalized, and generally more benevolent, form of an activity that takes place under the state's radar in almost every society. Informal moneylenders, or loan sharks as they are sometimes called, are common throughout the world. This makes microfinance a unique and interesting approach to poverty alleviation that may or may not coincide with the patterns seen with aid, FDI, and other types of programs.

This uniquely individualist approach has captured the attention of economic liberals from around the world. It does not depend on taxpayer-funded government programs; it does not depend on the steady flow of charitable donations; and it does not depend on pyramid schemes or anything else. At its root, microfinance relies on a well-recognized, tried and tested model. It depends on individuals being clever and innovative, taking risks with an entrepreneurial spirit. In short, it is western liberal economics, scaled down and repackaged to account for the unique challenges facing the poor in developing countries. At least, that is the way many advocates see it.

Skeptics see it as a thinly veiled attempt to twist and repackage an economic system that has already failed the poor in order to exploit them (Bateman 2010). For some, microfinance, especially profit-oriented microfinance, is an inexcusable exploitation of the poor. These ruinously high interest rates are unheard of in the developed world, but the poorest people in the poorest countries are expected to pay the astronomical rates and to be grateful for the chance to do so, if it means access to credit. Microfinance customers may be going hungry in order to pay interest that will earn fat cats at the top millions of dollars. The disparity is jarring for some.

## HOW MICROFINANCE WORKS

To help the reader understand some of the nuances of microfinance and its evolution, this section describes in broad brush strokes the major actors, processes and organizations generally involved. Beginning in 1974 Muhammad Yunus and the Grameen Bank started fighting poverty in Bangladesh with a different approach than was typical at the time, by offering financial services to households deemed unworthy of credit by commercial institutions or those who could not afford to pay commercial fees. The expansion of financial services to the poor, now widely referred to as microfinance, quickly saw tremendous success in Bangladesh and was rapidly exported to a number of other countries. Logic suggests that if the poor can obtain lump sums of money in order to take advantage of opportunities when they arise, their quality of life will improve. For a time microfinance seemed to be a panacea, and a group of literature popped up singing praises of its ability to fight poverty, with titles like *Fighting Poverty with Microcredit* (Khandker 1998), *Microfinance and Poverty Alleviation* (Remenyi and Quinones 2000) and *The Poor Always Pay Back* (Dowla and Barua 2006). The microfinance movement received great distinction in 2006 when Yunus was awarded the Nobel Peace Prize for his work that started with the Grameen Bank.[4] Over the last few years, however, scholars have begun to question both the exportability and the depth of the success reported in the microfinance literature (Brau and Woller 2004; Ault and Spicer 2009).

As mentioned above, some of the problems microfinance faces are that the poor generally have no collateral for loans, cannot afford the fees required for most formal financial services, and often carry out a lot of their economic activity in the grey market, so there is no record of income or credit. Nevertheless, building or buying houses, paying for education, or building a micro-enterprise requires an accumulation of capital that a poor household might not be able to achieve on its own, even when the payoff for doing so might be significant (Aghion and Morduch 2005). Formal financial institutions often have little or no information about the risks associated with lending to individuals in these conditions because, for example, there are no credit history agencies. Even if the lender knew something about the borrower's credit worthiness, the loan sizes would be so small as to be unprofitable following a traditional commercial lending model. Yunus and the Grameen Bank, and many other microfinance institutions (MFIs), have developed solutions to work around these problems in order to make financial services for the poor at least sustainable, so that they do not have to rely on continual infusions of capital, and are perhaps even profitable.

One approach often relied on by microfinance lenders is to lend to groups. The loan agent goes to a village and offers a small loan to a group of between five and fifteen individuals with a promise that if it is repaid on time, another, larger, loan will be dispersed to the group, followed by another and another according to the group's needs. The catch is that the lender loans money to one person in the group at a time, and the rest of the group only get their loan in due course and if all previous borrowers of the group have repaid their loans on time. The benefit of this approach is that the villagers have much better information about who can be trusted. This takes the burden of credit monitoring and background checks off the lender and puts it onto the group. The group is able to shoulder the burden rather easily because in a small village everybody knows everybody else and they all have a pretty good idea of who they can trust and who they can work with (Aghion and Morduch 2005).

Group lending addresses another obstacle that gets in the way of traditional finance. A commercial bank would have no leverage over a borrower if he had no collateral to put against the loan. But, by lending to a group and conditioning other group members' loans on each person's timely repayment, the lender is effectively holding the borrower's social capital with the rest of the group as collateral. Social capital is highly valuable among the poor, who often rely on family, friends and neighbors in times of need, and leveraging social capital has been quite effective. Indeed, some MFIs see repayment rates exceeding 98%, which is higher than many traditional financial institutions in wealthy countries (Dowla and Barua 2006).

Another approach is to require a customer to make minimum deposits into a savings account for some period of time, before extending a loan, to show that they are reliable and capable of making payments. Then the lender holds the savings until the borrower repays the loan, at which time the savings are again made available to the borrower. This doubles the effect of the loan since the customer gets the loan money and the savings in lump sums, while also giving the lender a degree of collateral against default. The lump sums allow the customer to make the big purchases that are likely to improve her income or quality of life.

In a similar vein, MFIs generally require regular repayments, which might begin as little as one week after the loan is disbursed. This is said to help the borrower to be financially disciplined, since the customer has to save a small amount of money every week or two to pay installments (Aghion and Morduch 2005). Presumably this is easier for the borrower than saving the money on their own and paying it all back in a lump sum when the loan comes due, as might happen with a loan shark, or even paying just monthly. These are not strict models, of course, but examples of the mechanisms that MFIs have developed and implemented. Most MFIs mix and match the various mechanisms to serve their and their customers' needs.

Early successes reported by the Grameen Bank in Bangladesh and by BancoSol in Bolivia led to something of a microfinance revolution. Today there are MFIs across the world. They take various shapes. Some look and function similarly to the early Grameen Bank, while others, including the Grameen Bank itself, have undergone significant innovations, adopting and adapting the various mechanisms to achieve their objectives. They continue to evolve in order to better serve their customers' needs and to operate more efficiently.

While some MFIs remain non-profit organizations, many for-profit MFIs have entered the market too. This is one of the more important distinctions among MFIs. Either not-for-profits keep interest rates and fees just high enough to cover costs, or they dump all of their revenue back into loans in order to extend outreach or cover loan loss. Both NGOs and governments might run these institutions. For-profit MFIs tend to have higher interest rates and fees, which put more of a burden on the customers who are already at or near poverty levels, but they also fill a niche in the market, since investors can put money into MFIs that will return a profit. This allows them to expand more quickly and opens doors for commercial sources of funding that might not be available to non-profit MFIs. There are pros and cons to each of these, and they often exist simultaneously in any given state or region, depending on government regulations and the market (more on this in chapter 2).

With all of these innovations, microfinance has gained acclaim and recognition in the development community as a useful tool for fighting poverty. TheMIX.org, a non-profit organization that collects data on MFIs for policy makers and researchers to use, reports data for over 2000 MFIs in 67 countries. It estimates that the global gross loan portfolio for microfinance was over $65 billion in 2009 (theMIX.org). Considering that many people had not even heard of microfinance up to 2000, this represents tremendous growth. The growth and popularity of the industry has been helped along by the United Nations' *Year of Microcredit* in 2005, and Yunus's and the Grameen Bank's joint Nobel Prize in 2006.

Microfinance has caught on among the public in wealthy countries too. Kiva.org, for example, makes it possible for anybody to lend money to a microfinance project. The organization collects stories about their borrowers, or entrepreneurs as they are called by the organization, so that lenders can see to whom the money is going. This approach has been quite successful. Kiva has attracted over a million lenders who have jointly lent out nearly five hundred million dollars in zero interest loans since the organization was founded in 2005.[5]

In spite of all of the innovations and adaptations in microfinance over the years, or perhaps because of them, not all ventures are successful. Depending on the definition of success, there are numerous examples to illustrate this. The stories presented at the beginning of the chapter illustrate one failure to improve the quality of life of a customer. Some studies suggest that Razia's story is not uncommon, or at least that Murshida's story is not necessarily the norm. Microfinance may fail at the institutional level or at the state level, as happened in Thailand or Andhra Pradesh in India when loan write-offs skyrocketed and the entire industry nearly collapsed (Mahajan 2007; Islam 2009; Imai, Arun, and Annim 2010; Roodman 2012). This project will advance our understanding of microfinance.

## RESEARCH QUESTION

Microfinance is an appealing poverty alleviation mechanism for several reasons. First, it is based on the neoclassical growth model which suggests that if an economy has a lot of labor and not very much capital, an influx of capital should boost productivity and increase incomes (Easterly 2001). Imagine two construction companies, one in the US and one in Guatemala. The US company excavates construction sites with front loaders, dump trucks and graders. The Guatemalan company has one small, worn out backhoe and a pickup with a trailer, and dozens of employees with shovels and wheelbarrows. The US-based company may increase its production efficiency by purchasing new front loader tractors that can scoop up five cubic yards of material at a time, compared to the old machines that could only do three yards at a time. Each machine costs tens of thousands of dollars and will increase worker productivity by two-thirds in one stage of the excavation process. The Guatemalan company can spend a few thousand dollars to buy some used, old-model equipment and increase productivity by ten times. Without taking into account the political and economic environment, the same lump of cash should have a much greater impact in Guatemala compared to the US because the US is capital rich and Guatemala is capital poor. This is why many people expect microfinance to have such a large impact on the people and economies of developing countries. The influx of capital should allow those who are capital poor to significantly increase their productivity.

There are numerous stories, whether real or not, of microfinance customers who were sewing clothes by hand, but once they received a microloan were able to buy a sewing machine, or make some other equally impactful investment. The machine increased their productivity so much that they were able to quickly repay the loan and significantly increase their income. Indeed, making labor more productive is a key part of the development process. If microloans accelerate that process and make it available to whoever is clever enough and determined enough to make a go of it, even if they are desperately poor, then it is a socially and economically attractive program.

Second, microfinance skirts government involvement. Taxpayers tire of hearing about waste and corruption scandals in foreign aid projects. They feel like their hard-earned tax dollars are being squandered by elites in poor countries. Afghanistan, for example, is perceived to have the fourth most corrupt government in the world, according to Transparency International's 2014 survey. Despite the corruption, the US government gave Afghanistan more than $2.5 billion in 2014. Many people in developed countries have some degree of compassion for the poor in developing countries, but they chafe when they learn that aid is being wasted through incompetence or stolen by corrupt officials.[6] If it were possible to cut government out of the process, then corrupt elites would not have a chance to pilfer money intended for the poor. Citizens of developed countries could feel better about allocating their money to such a project and the poor of developing countries would see a larger portion of cash. Microfinance's detachment from government makes it unique among poverty alleviation mechanisms.

Third, microfinance is an individualistic approach to poverty alleviation. It is a chance to have the American Dream anywhere in the world. It appeals to the Protestant work ethic common in many western societies; people can improve their station in life if they just work hard enough and lift themselves up by their bootstraps. It rewards hard work and independence without supporting moochers. It offers people a hand up, rather than a handout. This appeals politically to many people in the developed world who want to help the poor but who fear that aid donations can perpetuate entitlement or dependence. The notion that microfinance recipients are being given a temporary boost that will help them to be self-sufficient also looks like a viable solution to a long-standing problem.

Despite the popular appeal of microfinance, there are still many things we do not know about it. Perhaps the most important question that most people do not realize has yet to be definitively answered is whether microfinance actually reduces poverty at all. Experts have been arguing this point for several years now, but the debate is far from over. This has already come up, but chapter 2 will go into greater detail. Second is whether there are particular conditions that make it more or less effective. The empirical puzzle that is driving this project stems from the observation that microfinance appears to be quite successful in some cases, but not in others. For example, it seems to work in most of Bangladesh particularly under the BRAC, a development NGO. However, it appears to have failed miserably in other places, such as northern Thailand, which despite having considerable access to financial services for the poor has seen no improvement in poverty rates or quality of life among the poor (Imai, Arun, and Annim 2010).

Looking at this problem as a political scientist, it seems likely that despite microfinance being relatively independent from government, it is still influenced by the macro environment that governments create. I suspect that government plays a significant role by implementing policies and agreements that shape the regulations and the market for microfinance. The primary question this book tries to answer, then, is "how does the government affect the ability of MFIs to reduce poverty?" This question can be divided into two distinct questions, but it also spawns a number of corollary questions. First, the question might be reworded as "does better governance create economic conditions that make microfinance a more efficient mechanism for reducing poverty?" This question addresses where, or under what types of political conditions, a dollar of microfinance capital has the greatest impact on poverty reduction. This might be a question that a philanthropist asks herself when considering a donation to an MFI somewhere in the world if she wants her donation to have the largest impact possible on global poverty. Alternatively, an entrepreneur or financial firm considering opening a commercial MFI might be equally interested in the answer to this question. If microfinance has a larger impact on poverty in some countries than in others, it would have obvious implications for social activists and investors.

While some people focus on poverty reduction at the global level, others are interested in poverty reduction in a particular country. They might want to know how to reduce poverty in a specific region or state. For this group the original question might be reworded as "what policies can a government introduce to make microfinance more effective at reducing poverty within its borders?" In other words, the results of this study will have real world implications for philanthropists, investors, MFI managers, entrepreneurs and policy makers. Although microfinance has been found to be a useful tool for combating poverty in some cases, we need to understand it more thoroughly in order to use it effectively and efficiently. We have learned much since Yunus began making microloans in 1974, but there are still aspects about which we have little empirically substantiated understanding.

Many scholars have studied various aspects of microfinance, and several have even examined how government policies and bureaucracy might affect microfinance. The difference between those works and this one is that they have looked at things such as whether the MFIs or the microenterprises they finance were able to grow (Ault and Spicer 2009), or how efficiently the MFIs functioned in terms of repayment rates or other measures of the financial health of institutions rather than on whether they influenced quality of life for the poor (Duflos and Imboden 2003; Meagher et al. 2006). This project will focus specifically on how government policies and bureaucracy affect whether or not microfinance actually improves the lives of the poor.

This project has merit beyond the policy and business worlds too. Although there is a good body of research on microfinance in the development and growth literature, surprisingly little of it addresses how government regulations and bureaucracy affect the individual level impact of microfinance (*see* Haggard and Tiede 2011 *for an exception*). This project will add to the theoretical literature as it synthesizes across several disparate literatures to answer the questions raised above. It will bring together research from the governance and rule of law literature in political science, the growth and development literature, and the FDI literature from economics. It will also add to the body of empirical work on microfinance that is still trying to understand its impact more precisely.

The major theoretical contribution this book makes is to look at microfinance through the lens of a political scientist interested in governance and poverty alleviation. This will give me leverage over a problem that has some important real world implications for billions of people living below or near the poverty line around the globe and who might benefit from microfinancial services. Understanding what makes microfinance work and what does not makes it a more precise tool in the hands of policy makers and investors. The more information policy makers have about microfinance, the more effectively they can tailor policies that will encourage the efficient allocation of resources.

The research presented herein could lead to any of a handful of possible conclusions, each with its own implications for practitioners, policy makers and investors. One possible conclusion is that the state affects the poverty alleviation capabilities of microfinance, either positively or negatively. As indicated above, this would be an important finding because it might suggest where microfinance investments could be used most effectively for poverty alleviation and where other approaches might be efficacious. This is likely a complex set of relationships, though. This project would be the first deep plunge into understanding the intricacies of the conditions under which the relationships exist. It would almost certainly open up a fruitful avenue for future research. It might also help policy makers and NGOs, IGOs or partner states help shape policies and bureaucracy in a poor state to maximize poverty alleviation from microfinance.

Another potential outcome is that the state has no effect on microfinance. This would be a surprising result since virtually all other efforts at poverty alleviation are, at least somewhat, influenced by the state.[7] A finding that the state has no impact on whether microfinance affects poverty alleviation would present a shocking anomaly in the economic development and international political economy literatures, but would also make microfinance a uniquely useful tool for poverty alleviation. It is also possible that microfinance does not work. That is, it does not help alleviate poverty. This would be a game-changing result, considering how much money and how many organizations and individuals have contributed to microfinance under the premise that it helps the poor.

## STRUCTURE OF THE BOOK

The next chapter discusses several groups of literature that are related to the research question presented above. The first group of literature discusses previous research on microfinance, with an emphasis on impact studies. Many experts have examined the effect that microfinance has on the poor. Much of the literature has found that it is helpful, although some has found either no discernible effect or even a negative effect on the poor. This dichotomy is one of the primary motivations for this project. Other literatures discussed include risk and how it is used to understand decision making, the effect of political and economic instability on other poverty alleviation and development mechanisms, and Popkin's rational peasant argument, or the ability of the poor to make strategic decisions about their personal financial situations (Popkin 1979). Looking at the literature helps establish the intellectual platform created by years of research from dozens of experts, which serves as a jumping-off point for the rest of the book.

Chapter 3 presents a theory of the effects government and stability might have on the poverty reduction effect of microfinance. It first argues that microfinance should have at worst a neutral effect on poverty since the poor are not required to take loans and are only likely to do so if it improves their quality of life in some way. It then discusses how political institutions and political or economic instability might affect whether a microfinance borrower is actually able to improve her quality of life by taking advantage of microfinance services. It sets out three hypotheses to be tested in the subsequent chapters. The first is that microfinance should have a positive impact on poverty, regardless of political and economic stability. The second hypothesis is that political and economic stability should foster poverty alleviation, regardless of microfinance and other poverty alleviation efforts. Third, political stability and economic stability both should make microfinance operate more efficiently as a poverty alleviation mechanism.

Chapter 4 is the first empirical test of the theory. It examines a panel of all Latin American states for which there are data over a 20-year time period. It employs linear regression to determine whether there is support for the hypotheses developed in chapter 3. It discusses the data, where they came from, and why it is an appropriate test of the hypotheses. The results support the connection between microfinance and poverty reduction. Political conditions indeed seem to matter, as do economic and financial conditions, at least sometimes. In fact, political conditions may make the difference between microfinance reducing poverty and exacerbating poverty for some MFI customers.

Chapter 5 is a case study, which looks at the political developments in Brazil from approximately 1930 to the present. It discusses the conditions that have perpetuated poverty in Brazil and how those related to microfinance. It also explains the economic environment in Brazil when microfinance began to take hold on a large scale and how changes in the political and economic conditions appear to influence the relationship between microfinance and poverty reduction. This chapter also finds that the economic environment seems to be important, but less so for the political environment. The combination of the quantitative analysis of chapter 4 and the case study analysis in chapter 5 provides a useful mixed-methods look at microfinance in an important developing economy.

Chapter 6 looks at how microfinance is currently distributed. It discusses where funding for MFIs comes from and where it goes. It also looks at which states attract the most funding for their microfinance industry. It then compares the trends we observe to the conditions that make microfinance more effective. There are some states in which microfinance plays a much larger role than others. The current distribution of microfinance resources and MFIs themselves may be poorly distributed for poverty alleviation purposes. In fact, there are still some lingering doubts about whether microfinance, even under the best conditions, is a good investment relative to other poverty alleviation mechanisms. This chapter explores these debates and compares microfinance to conditional cash transfer programs, another poverty alleviation mechanism that has taken root in Brazil.

The final chapter summarizes the findings of this project. It then discusses the theoretical contributions of this project. These contributions include further evidence on the impact of microfinance, but, more importantly, it illustrates one reason that there may be discrepancies between others' findings. It also lends support to the rational peasant argument and those who suggest that development is best served when the poor are given the power to make choices. This chapter also points out the implications these findings might have for microfinance practitioners. The most obvious is that microfinance probably works better in some conditions than in others. It also suggests that microfinance providers might do well to expand risk reduction services, or insurance, and not just lending. The chapter concludes by discussing where future research might further our understanding of these phenomena.

## NOTES

1. This story and the next are both borrowed from David Roodman's (2012) book *Due Diligence: An Impertinent Inquiry into Microfinance*.

2. Within each of the eight general goals are specific, verifiable goals such as halving, between 1990 and 2015, the proportion of people whose income is less than $1.25 a day. We, as a global community, have achieved a few of the goals, such as reducing extreme poverty by half, and we have come very close to achieving others, like ensuring that, by 2015, children everywhere, boys and girls alike, will be able to complete a full course of primary schooling. On other goals we have made embarrassingly little progress, though. For example, the global community has made little headway in the last fifteen years on environmental issues. We are not much closer to curbing biodiversity loss than we were in 2000.

3. China eventually upped its aid offering to $1.6 million and a disaster relief team. To give some context, the US, whose economy was a little more than twice the size of China's at the time, committed $20 million to disaster relief.

4. Yunus was actually awarded the prize in conjunction with the Grameen Bank. However, since it was largely his efforts that created the bank, some people see little distinction between Yunus and the bank he created.

5. Kiva loans are zero interest for the lender, but not for the borrower. Borrowers still pay normal interest rates and the MFIs actually reap the rewards.

6. It is difficult to know how much aid is lost due to corruption for at least two reasons. First, those who are taking money by corrupt means do their best to hide it. Second, aid is generally fungible. Imagine that illicit outflows from country X are $10 million one year. The following year, country X receives a $5 million aid package, and illicit outflows grow by $2 million. That does not necessarily mean that 40% of

the aid package was lost to corruption. There are too many other factors that might drive illicit outflows. So, if the government in country X can show that all five million was spent on building schools, but its own budget for building schools dropped from two million to one million, it's difficult to classify that as corruption.

7. The popular titles by well-known economists mentioned earlier all give some attention to the functioning of the state, as do many other academic and policy oriented research papers.

## Chapter Two

# What We Know So Far

The research question relates to several other areas of research. While this project is distinctive in its focus and approach, the main themes to be addressed here have been studied by many scholars and experts before, and this project is a piece of a much larger puzzle. One of the primary themes is, of course, microfinance. Though microfinance has only really been a global phenomenon since the 1990s, it has garnered a lot of attention and has been examined from three general perspectives. These include the repayment of microloans, the potential for profitable microfinance and the effect microfinance has on poverty. All three are often spoken of as the rubric for successful microfinance, and sometimes even treated as synonymous, though they are not always correlated, as this and subsequent chapters will show. Each of these will be discussed in turn. The second topic deals with other poverty alleviation and development mechanisms, and, more precisely, how they are affected by government institutions, or the lack thereof. Microfinance may be different from other poverty alleviation programs, but it is necessary to understand those differences and similarities before examining the impact they might have on outcomes. The final topic has its roots in Samuel Popkin's rational peasants theory and deals with the economic decisions of the poor (Popkin 1979). First, though, it is necessary to clarify some terms.

## KEY TERMS AND CONCEPTS

There are some key terms and concepts that came up in the first chapter and which will continue to appear throughout the rest of this work. They are common terms, though used with specific meanings here. Before moving into a discussion of the model itself, this section will discuss these terms and their precise meanings for this study.

The first term is government. When government is mentioned herein, it is a reference to the ruling authority of the state, generally with references to the actions taken by said party. Political scientists and economists often use the term "governance," as evidenced by the World Bank's data set of World Governance Indicators; a group of indicators that generally measure the quality or functioning of the bureaucracy in a state. These indicators include measures of the rule of law and functioning of the courts. These are precisely the things that might affect microfinance and poverty. However, in the microfinance literature governance often refers to an MFI's management and leadership (Thapa 2010; Roodman 2012). For this book, "governance" is used in the traditional political science context and not the microfinance industry jargon.

Microfinance, another term that deserves some clarification, is the provision of financial services on a smaller scale than traditional financial institutions are generally interested in accommodating. Since poor households in developing countries have small incomes and typically deal with small amounts of money, the small-scale financial services that meet their needs have been dubbed *micro*finance. Although the early roots of the microfinance movement were often called micro-credit, and focused on non-profit organizations making small, short-term loans to groups of people, microfinance has evolved considerably. MFIs today often accept or even require customers' deposits into a savings account. Some offer forms of insurance, education and health care to their customers as well. Moreover, MFIs today might choose to offer loans on an individual basis, or for terms that go well beyond a few weeks or months as in the early days of the Grameen Bank (Aghion and Morduch 2005; Dowla and Barua 2006; Collins et al. 2009). Another significant shift includes the rising involvement of for-profit organizations in the microfinance industry. Some commercial banks and other types of investors have begun establishing operations in the microfinance sector and earn profits by doing so.[1] While lending is still the primary activity of most MFIs, it is all part of microfinance.

The third term is poverty reduction. In the economics and political science literatures, not to mention the policy world, there are many measures and definitions of poverty. Some rely on thresholds that cut across cultural divisions, economic variations and all other differences, such as the one dollar per person per day threshold. The precise measurement of poverty is an issue for the next chapter; suffice it to say that the poor are those who struggle to meet basic needs, such as sufficient nutrition, clean water, clothing and shelter. There is little dispute about who scholars are talking about when they mention the poor, but there is more disagreement about what poverty reduction means. Some focus exclusively on economic characteristics such as whether a family lives on less than $1/day per person. In this study I take poverty reduction to include anything that improves the quality of life of the poor, or even the near poor. I prefer a broad understanding because much of the economic life of the poor, especially those in poorer countries, occurs in the grey market where it is difficult or impossible to track by quantitative statistics. Also, it is easy to imagine mechanisms for improving the quality of life of an individual without changing her economic status. For example, smoothing a person's income reduces the temptation to spend extra income during good times and the stress of finding food during difficult times. Improving health might not have any discernible effect on a person's income, but most people would agree that feeling physically well improves quality of life. It is not difficult to think of many more examples.

## MICROFINANCE

Before Yunus created the Grameen Bank, commercial lending institutions did not lend to the poor for two reasons. First, it was unprofitable. The poor did not need or want large loans. By the time the bank paid a loan officer to process the loan application for the small loan a poor borrower might be interested in, the cost of processing the loan was more than the profit from interest on the loan was worth (Aghion and Morduch 2005). Banks would lose money by making micro loans to the poor, even assuming away all default. However, the poor still could benefit from financial services and even wanted financial services, if they could be accessed at the right price. The traditional finance market failed to meet that demand.

The second reason banks did not lend to the poor was that there was no guarantee that the impoverished borrower would repay the loan. Credit rating agencies in developing countries often have spotty coverage. In most low-income and many middle-income countries credit monitoring does not cover the poor because it is not financially lucrative and because the poor operate so much in the informal economy. Either way, banks likely have no reliable way of knowing what sort of credit history a potential borrower from a poor household might have. Moreover, without a credit history that would reflect whether the borrower defaulted on the loan, the bank assumed, perhaps wisely, that the borrower would have no incentive to repay the loan.

It is possible to overcome this lack of information if the borrower has collateral she can offer against the loan. In that case, the borrower is essentially paying a fee to turn a non-liquid asset temporarily into a liquid asset. This is virtually impossible for the poor in most developing countries because they, of course, have very few possessions. For those few possessions they do have that might be valuable enough to be acceptable as collateral, such as a house, the poor household likely has no proof of legal ownership, or, perhaps, any legal rights (Galiani and Schargrodsky 2010). Therefore, the poor effectively have no credit history to show that they are reliable borrowers or that can be damaged if they default. Nor do they have any collateral a bank could hold against a loan in the event of default. Clearly, then, banks have no incentive to offer credit to the poor. They cannot make any money on it, and they have no reason to believe that the borrower would not default.

Microfinance institutions have come up with clever ways to deal with these problems, as described previously. Some of these methods include group lending to people from the same village or neighborhood who know each other's financial situations, forced savings that are relinquished upon repayment, and graduated loan schemes to encourage repayment. One of the early questions, though, was whether these approaches to lending worked. Consequently, much of the microfinance literature is devoted to addressing this question by looking at repayment rates or return borrower rates to try and understand the conditions under which borrowers were likely to repay loans (Collins et al. 2009; Dowla and Barua 2006; Field and Pande 2007; Hermes and Lensink 2007; Hulme and Arun 2011; Marconi and Mosley 2006; Remenyi and Quinones 2000; Shoji 2010). The consensus is that, given a properly administered MFI, microfinance borrowers consistently repay their loans, and often at higher rates than in the general consumer credit market.

The darker side of this, however, is that there are many stories of MFI collectors putting great pressure on borrowers to repay their loans, greater pressure even than a commercial bank might put on a defaulting borrower (Roodman 2012). If the loan did not increase household income, or the family ran into trouble trying to repay the loan for some other reason, the constant pressure from hard-driving collectors may lead families to miss meals, sell appliances or forgo medical treatments in order to pay off the loan. Debtors are regularly arrested in some countries, which sparked widespread protests against microfinance and a microfinance crisis in Nicaragua in 2008. It is also disappointingly common to see reports of suicides that were provoked by the inability to repay loans (Hulme 2000).

Also, because microloans are often disbursed to social groups, and others' loans may be conditioned on repayment of all group members, if a borrower finds herself in a position where she is unable to make payments on her loan she may be socially ostracized from the rest of the group. This is, potentially, far more damaging to personal well-being than a poor credit history. Social groups are often relied on to help with financial stability, emotional and material support in both the normal day-to-day as well as major life events, such as a birth or a death. Eroding the social fabric of a small community may impose long-lasting costs on the delinquent debtor that spill over into the rest of the community.

It is worth mentioning here that microfinance debtors do not have the same legal protections for unforeseen financial hardships that debtors in developed countries often have. If either a household or a business takes a loan from a commercial borrower in the US, for example, if that debtor should meet financial hardship and finds herself unable to repay the loan, she can file for bankruptcy protection. There are multiple types of bankruptcy protection that can be tailored to individual circumstances. For example, when a small business files for bankruptcy, it protects the debtor's personal assets from seizure. The logic for this is that offering some degree of protection helps ameliorate risk and incentivizes innovation and entrepreneurialism (Chang 2012). Microfinance debtors are not afforded the same protections. They must bear the full cost of any risk or financial failure that might occur.

## For-Profit versus Non-Profit

Another big question in the microfinance literature is whether microfinance could become first sustainable, and then profitable. Many of the first MFIs, such as the Grameen Bank in Bangladesh or Banco do Nordeste in Brazil, were started either by government actors or other non-profit entities (Duflos and Imboden 2003; Mukherjee 1997). This, in and of itself, is not necessarily a problem. The problem comes from being able to scale up. Assuming that lack of capital is a major impediment to offering financial services to more people around the world, if the only actors who have incentives, or are permitted to open and operate MFIs, are non-profit actors, that severely limits the number of entities that might be willing to engage in micro-lending. Therefore, extending microfinance outreach becomes a difficult proposition. Also, if it falls to governments to create and operate MFIs, those countries most in need of poverty relief would be the ones least likely to get it, since the states with the worst poverty problems often have governments that are either incapable of or uninterested in addressing poverty.

This would then leave it up to non-governmental organizations (NGOs) such as the Grameen Foundation, or inter-governmental organizations (IGOs) such as the Inter-American Development Bank to create and operate all of the MFIs. The number of these organizations is somewhat limited and their resources are generally quite restricted since they both rely on donations. So expanding the number and scope of MFIs to be able to offer financial services to the poor all over the world would be out of the question due to the dearth of operators and funds. Moreover, NGOs are limited by the interests of their donors, since they cannot operate without funds from their donors, and IGOs are limited by the interests of their member states. Either scenario may curtail microfinance outreach.

Also, although group lending makes up some of the difference between loan processing costs and interest earned on micro-loans by processing several loans for little more effort than processing a single loan, group lending has its limits. It quickly became apparent that trying to lend to too large a group caused more problems than it solved (Aghion and Morduch 2005; Roodman 2012). So, this problem left two avenues open. MFIs could charge enough interest and fees on their loans to cover their lending and operating costs or they could remain dependent on donations and contributions from third parties. The latter option would mean that scaling up microfinance would be very difficult, since it would depend, once again, on donations (Copestake 2007).

The other option, to charge higher interest and fees, has its own problems. While this approach would allow MFIs to operate without being dependent on continued donations, thereby allowing them to expand regardless of external support, the annualized interest rates might have to be as high as 80% APR, or more, to cover costs (Roodman 2012).[2] It is important to remember that most of these loans are short-term loans, often with loan periods of just a few months. This means borrowers are not actually repaying the loans 1.8 times, but having to pay that kind of interest would severely cut into any economic advancement a borrower might make. In other words, a lot of people have argued that for-profit microfinance is usury and is just another way the rich are trying to get richer off the backs of the poor (Schicks 2007; Bateman 2010). While this is, perhaps, not an unfair critique, making microfinance profitable may be the most viable way to create a microfinance industry that has a chance of growing to meet global demand and thereby reach the millions of poor who do not currently have access to financial services.

The question many researchers asked, though, is whether charging those sorts of interest rates, considered usurious in commercial banking, would deter the poor from borrowing (Demirgüç-Kunt and Morduch 2011; Imai, Arun, and Annim 2010; Mahajan 2007). The answer is clearly that it does not. For-profit MFIs have plenty of customers. On the other hand, they also might not be reaching out to the poorest of the poor because the MFI is looking for larger returns (Imai, Arun, and Annim 2010). There are even allegations that some for-profit MFIs provide loans to poor borrowers without helping them to understand the full cost of the loans and using hard-sell tactics to move more loans. The benefit of for-profit microfinance is that it draws in far more capital for microfinance operations than non-profit lenders can. More capital, of course, means greater outreach and more people who are offered access to microfinance. The drawback of for-profit microfinance is that it is even more expensive than loans from non-profit lenders because somebody is making money off the poor. In the case of Compartamos, for example, some people were making a tremendous amount of money off loans to the poor (Bateman 2010).

As microfinance became more popular in development circles, Yunus and other microfinance advocates and practitioners offered convincing anecdotes of people dramatically improving their quality of life by having access to financial services. An example is the story of Murshida told at the beginning of chapter 1. Some people seemed to take it for granted that microfinance reduced poverty. Of course, stories of disappointment, like Razia's, eventually surfaced too, so researchers began questioning whether microfinance is actually beneficial. On the one hand, there are a number of case studies which show that microfinance can be very beneficial (Beck, Demirgüç-Kunt, and Levine 2007; Dupas and Robinson 2010; Gulyani and Talukdar 2010; Imai et al. 2012; Islam 2009; Montgomery and Weiss 2011; Odell 2011; Remenyi and Quinones 2000). On the other hand, there are also a number of studies that do not find convincing evidence that microfinance is beneficial (Karlan and Zinman 2009; Navajas et al. 2000). Still others find that it might be helpful, but only under specific and limited conditions (Duvendack et al. 2011; Hulme and Arun 2011; Mahajan 2007; Roodman 2012); and some which find that microfinance might be harmful to the poor (Roodman 2012; Bateman 2010).

## POLITICAL AND ECONOMIC STABILITY

The third major theme discussed in this work is the effect of governance and political or economic stability on poverty alleviation and development efforts. This is the source of risk which might affect potential microfinance customers' decisions. Few researchers have written about the effects of poor governance on microfinance, but there is a strong body of research dealing with how instability affects economic growth, foreign aid, and foreign direct investment. There is a mountain of evidence showing that instability inhibits economic growth and interferes with the effectiveness of poverty alleviation efforts (Chauvet and Guillamont 2004; Chong, Gradstein, and Calderon 2009).

Political stability appears to influence foreign aid effectiveness through fungibility. This is the ability of the recipient government to divert its own resources away from programs that would promote development or economic growth and substitute its own spending with outside resources coming in as aid packages. Leaders might do this in order to shore up the state in other areas, or, more likely, to line elites' pockets. In other cases, when states face social instability they address it by expanding government to create a vast bureaucracy that allows many actors to skim off the top. Allowing more actors to engage in rent-seeking behavior may placate enough people to forestall more serious instability. The problem for aid is that with so many actors skimming off the top, those individuals have little incentive to innovate and grow the economy since they can just engage in rent-seeking behavior. The rest of society has little ability to innovate because all of the skimming leaves little profit for the producer (Hubbard and Duggan 2009). It might also simply be that those states which tend to be susceptible to instability also often suffer from corruption, which eats away at people's incentives to innovate and to try and improve their economic situation because they are able to keep only a relatively small portion of their economic output (Collier 2007; Easterly 2001; Easterly 2006; Hunt and Laszlo 2012).

While foreign aid is probably the development mechanism that most people are familiar with, the potential economic growth and poverty reduction effects of FDI are more relevant to the research question than is foreign aid. Foreign direct investors are profit-driven actors who carefully study the political and economic climate of a country in which they have or are considering an investment, in order to manage their risk portfolio. FDI ranges from Chinese mining operations buying property in Africa, to Apple's association with Foxconn in China, or the auto companies building factories around the world. In some industries there is a significant efficiency advantage to having a portion of a production process in another country (Balaam and Dillman 2009). This might be because wages or taxes are lower there, or perhaps because it is closer to key production inputs, or for any number of other reasons. There is always a possibility that those advantages could be erased by unfavorable economic or political conditions. For example, if exchange rates swing wildly between the investor's home state and the target state, a rather profitable FDI prospect could quickly turn into an unprofitable investment. The risks of something like government appropriation of an industry, a conflict that shuts down production, or an inadequate response to a natural disaster could all have a major impact on the profitability of FDI. Consequently, numerous studies have found that FDI is sensitive to stability (Busse and Hefeker 2007; Daude and Stein 2007; Kolstad and Villanger 2008; Dutta and Roy 2011). Other studies find that FDI is sensitive to the quality of institutions in the target state (Globerman and Shapiro 2002; Li and Resnick 2003).

An extreme example of this phenomenon is when a state expropriates the holdings of a foreign firm. In some historical cases states have simply taken control of entire industries, often with little or no compensation for foreign investors' losses. During the first half of the twentieth century, the US was heavily involved in the Cuban economy. US firms invested in Cuba and many Americans traveled to and owned property in Cuba. When Castro's government expropriated foreign-held firms and properties after the Cuban Revolution ended in 1959, the Foreign Claims Settlement Commission created by the US Congress certified that US firms and American citizens lost a total of nearly $7.5 billion worth of assets (Travieso-Diaz 1995).[3]

While the likelihood of a government expropriating foreign firms is relatively low, it has happened and could happen again. More importantly, it illustrates the risk for foreign investors. A more likely example is civil war. In Collier's *The Bottom Billion*, he discusses poverty traps that inhibit economic growth (Collier 2007). Some research suggests that civil war reduces economic growth by about 2.3% per year on average (Haggard and Tiede 2011). That means at the end of a seven-year war, the economy will be 16% smaller that it would have been with no war. For states with otherwise strong economies, this makes for rather modest growth. States experiencing civil war are more likely to have relatively weak economies already, so civil war may well put the economy into recession or depression. Wars cause massive damage and destruction of physical capital, human capital, the natural environment and the social environment, not to mention the opportunity cost of fighting rather than producing (Lewis 1999). Collier provides a startling perspective on ubiquity of wars in the poorest of the poor states. Dividing history up into five-year segments, a poor state, or what Collier calls a Bottom Billion state, has a one in six chance of experiencing war in a five-year period (Collier 2007).

Another of Collier's poverty traps is the natural resource trap. This occurs when a state relies on natural resource extraction as an easy source of revenue. It requires little investment in human capital or infrastructure, and has the potential to pay big dividends. It also tends to subject the economy to great instability because the national economy relies so heavily on just a few outputs and natural resource markets often experience wild swings in prices (Balaam and Dillman 2009). It is lucrative to be a major exporter of a natural resource when commodity prices are high, but when prices slump it can be economically devastating. Many developing countries rely heavily on natural resource extraction to provide government revenue and jobs for citizens, but fluctuating commodity prices can make them vulnerable to severe economic instability. When commodity prices are high, it inflates the domestic currency, making manufacturers' exports unprofitable, and when commodity prices are low and government budgets suffer, the government might resort to cutting back port authority personnel, cutting energy subsidies, or to other potentially damaging policies.

Institutions affect economic growth too. For example, Rodrik and Wacziarg find that democracy promotes economic growth because it reduces uncertainty by taking the jumpiness out of the growth curve (2005). It is not uncommon to see poorly governed states experience spurts of economic growth intermingled with recessions. An example is the Brazilian growth miracle from 1967 to 1973 during which time Brazil was under military rule. The economy grew at double digit rates for six years before it began to fizzle, then, eventually, plummeted into a decade of abysmal economic performance. So, it seems that institutions are not always necessary for short-term economic growth, but sustained economic growth is rather unlikely without good institutions (Green 2011; Rodrik 2008). To be fair, improving institutions will only help in states where the quality of institutions is the constraining factor.

These are all things that investors consider before committing to FDI. Microfinance is different from FDI, but there are similarities too. Where FDI has to make a profit to survive as a business, MFI customers have to make a profit or earn wages in order to meet their minimum basic needs. FDI suffers when jumpy prices make key production inputs ruinously expensive, as do microenterprises. Where FDI might be harmed by lack of access to effective government services such as port authorities, microentrepreneurs might be harmed by excessive bureaucracy or rent-seeking. Microenterprises might, like FDI, be affected by instability in wages or the demand for labor as it affects potential customers' demand for the product the microenterprise is selling.

The well-demonstrated connection between political and economic stability on the one hand and the amount and profitability of FDI on the other hand is intuitive. Instinctively, it seems that the same connection likely exists for microfinance, but there is very little research that looks carefully at this phenomenon. Where political stability is a concern at all, the research generally focuses on its impacts on the MFI itself, and not on the households who take out microloans to try and improve their quality of life. One of the things that has made microfinance popular is its connection to corporate social responsibility, poverty alleviation and development. However, very little research has examined the connection between government, the single most important variable in the microfinance equation outside of the MFI and the client, and the impact microfinance has on poverty alleviation efforts. The connections between microfinance and corporate social responsibility, poverty alleviation and development are assumed, but largely unsubstantiated by research, especially in regard to the role government plays in these relationships. This stands as a glaring gap in the current literature.

## RATIONAL PEASANTS

The final area of previous work that is relevant to this research examines the business and investment acumen of the poor. Samuel Popkin wrote that peasants are rational actors who are driven by financial well-being rather than social or cultural ties (Popkin 1979). Popkin's peasants are analogous to potential and actual microfinance customers. When Popkin wrote in 1979, he was trying to debunk a long-standing claim that peasants were more concerned with maintaining their culture than with pursuing economic gains. The basis of his argument was that peasants are rational and intelligent enough to know that when they do not have other prospects, their best option is to rely on the communal village structure to ensure the well-being of the group. However, when a better opportunity arises, a peasant will abandon the other villagers in pursuit of her own economic interests. This line of argument contradicted previous literature, which claimed that villagers put great value on the communal village structure, and it was only influence from outside, what scholars today might call globalization, which caused villagers to cut their ties and adopt a new, independent financial path. The basic premise of this argument is that peasants, who are generally not very well educated, would be able to make these kinds of decisions with enough accuracy to be of benefit.

The essence of Popkin's argument is that peasants are rational, economically motivated actors. In other words, peasants are rational consumers and strategic investors. This idea agrees with the basic premise of microfinance, that the poor are able to make strategic decisions about their financial situations and prospects. Some poverty alleviation and development approaches do not make this assumption. Foreign aid, for example, does not put the onus of rational decision making on the poor. It relies, instead, on decision makers within the governments of the donor state and the recipient state to make the decisions about the application of those resources. This is where Easterly argues that aid tends to fail (Easterly 2006). Decision makers at the governmental level, whether in the donor state or the recipient state, have a terrible track record for making decisions about the allocation of resources in order to bring about discernible improvements in the quality of life or economic well-being of the poor on a large scale. Likewise, FDI, when directed to a less-developed state, generally reserves decision making for the wealthy investors from a developed state (Busse and Hefeker 2007).

The basic premise of microfinance, on the other hand, is that the poor are intelligent enough, and educated enough, to make efficient financial decisions. This is an idea that numerous scholars have embraced. Amartya Sen, the Nobel laureate in economics, argued on many occasions that freedom is key for development (Sen 2001). Sen argued that true development occurs when people in poor countries are given the opportunity to pursue their own best interests. When people have the freedom to pursue their personal political interests, as in a democracy, they choose leaders who champion their causes. In the same fashion, people who have the freedom to access financial services, to borrow money in order to start or expand a microenterprise, or to invest in human capital or in making a home operate more efficiently, will improve their own productivity and their quality of life. After all, nearly every person and virtually every country was dismally poor just a few hundred years ago, relative to today's standards (Easterly 2001). Many of them were able to rapidly increase their incomes rather quickly at some point. It seems reasonable, then, to assume that peasants in Thai villages or the poorer classes in Latin American societies might be able to do the same when the constraints on their economic productivity are alleviated. Microfinance is an attempt to alleviate what might be a constraint for many people in developing countries by providing them opportunities to expand their growth potential beyond what their present incomes allow by leveraging their income. After all, leveraging is how the wealthy generally increase their wealth.

Moreover, there is considerable evidence that the poor in modern societies are quite rational. Collins et al. (2009) conducted a study in which they tracked the financial transactions of poor households for approximately two years. Researchers asked each household in the study about their income, expenditures, and how they saved and borrowed money on a biweekly basis over the course of twelve to twenty-four months. One of their most important findings was that poor households in the countries they studied often engaged in rather complex financial interactions with friends, neighbors and family members, employers, retailers and occasionally loan sharks, in order to meet their financial needs. They point out that poor people in most countries are likely to have facilities in their towns or villages which provide public services, such as schools or health clinics. It is likely, though, that those public services do not function very well. Those same people are considerably less likely to have an institution in their municipality which offers financial services that they can access. "Microfinance's advantage in this race is that it can pursue the task of delivering reliable and affordable services to the poor independent of public resources. It can also operate with less dependence on political will" (Collins et al. 2009).

## CONCLUSION

The research question raised in the first chapter touches several fields of study. This chapter has presented and discussed the major connections to the different groups of previous research that are relevant to this project. The major groups of literature include previous research and approaches to studying microfinance, different ways of thinking about risk and how it affects decision making behavior, political and economic stability, and their relationship to poverty alleviation and development efforts, and, finally, the rational peasant argument and how it applies to microfinance.

The microfinance literature was divided into three groups. The early literature tended to focus on how to get loan money to people with no credit history and no collateral in such a way as to incentivize them to repay their loans. Another group of literature focused on the development of and differences between non-profit microfinance, as from an NGO, and profit-driven microfinance. The final group of microfinance literature, and the group that is most closely related to the research question here, addresses the impact of microfinance. It tries to determine whether or not microfinance improves the quality of life of the poor.

The last section of this chapter discussed Popkin's rational peasant argument and related it to a variety of development efforts (Popkin 1979). Some of these development efforts, such as foreign aid, give the decision making power to elites and policy makers. Microfinance, on the other hand, allows the poor to make the decisions about their own financial lives. This section also discussed the work of other scholars who have argued and shown that the latter approach may be more efficient.

## NOTES

1. These for-profit MFIs often have a "double bottom-line." That is, they are meant to be profitable, but that is not their only objective. They also try to improve the quality of life of the poor.

2. Compartamos is a Mexican bank and the largest microfinance bank in Latin America. The bank incorporated as a for-profit institution with an IPO (initial public offering) that netted hundreds of millions of dollars, dramatically enriching top executives. The bank also regularly charged interest rates over 100% APR for poor borrowers.

3. The figure is converted to 2013 constant dollars to account for inflation, but does not include interest on those assets.

# Chapter Three

# A Model of Poverty Reduction

This chapter sets out to develop and explain a model of how government bureaucracy and policies influence the microfinance industry within a state and the effects on poverty reduction. The model will then inform the empirical analyses in chapters 4 and 5. The model, once constructed, will reveal how I expect the various moving parts to fit together and interact with one another. More precisely, it will clearly explain how I believe government actions, or inactions, affect microfinance and poverty. By implication, it will also show where microfinance should be most effective based on the assumptions I employ.

## DEPARTING FROM PREVIOUS RESEARCH

This project jumps off from a platform created by other researchers. For example, researchers have shown that poor governance has a significant, negative effect on the impact of foreign aid. Significant instances of political instability, such as coups d'etat, decrease not only economic development but also the effectiveness of foreign aid and drive away FDI (Chauvet and Guillamont 2004; Hubbard and Duggan 2009). Foreign aid and FDI both suffer when corruption, ineffective or insufficient regulation, limited state capacity, and weak law and order are present in the state (Driver et al. 2004; Busse and Hefeker 2007; Daude and Stein 2007; Kolstad and Villanger 2008; Hunt and Laszlo 2012).

If foreign aid and FDI are both sensitive to government actions, it seems likely that microfinance should be as well. There are two ways of looking at this, though. On the one hand, microfinance is another financial mechanism that is intended, or attempting, to help the poor. On the other hand, microfinance is unique in that it occurs at the individual level, rather than the state level as with foreign aid and FDI. This unique feature casts doubt on the assertion that microfinance follows the same pattern as foreign aid and FDI.

Previous research has also made it clear that poverty reduction is an elusive objective. Quite often, millions of dollars are spent on aid with no perceptible change in poverty (Easterly 2006; Collier 2007; Hubbard and Duggan 2009). Researchers continue to try and understand why this is the case, but there seem to be a host of factors that impede poverty alleviation. Collier (2007) calls them the poverty traps; these are often structural characteristics that make development and economic growth nearly impossible. An example of such a characteristic is being land-locked with bad neighbors. Poor governance and recurring conflict also seem to inhibit economic success. Even where conditions seem to be ripe for economic growth, poverty alleviation and development still lie only along a hard-fought road (Dowla and Barua 2006; Moser 2007). In fact, despite the global community spending some $2.5 trillion on foreign aid since the 1940s, very few countries have broken loose from the poverty traps (Baker 2014).

Finally, recent research by Collins et al (2009) offers strong evidence that the poor need, and often use, financial services. In some cases they use it to smooth consumption when income is uneven, as for farmers who tend to receive income in lumps as the harvest is sold to the market, and even many factory workers whose industries experience waves of demand. They also use financial services to make large lump-sum purchases and even to invest money for the future, though there is some evidence that only a fraction of loans are actually used for productive purposes while the rest are used for consumer purchases (Bateman 2010). The poor do all of this while calculating their risks, if only crudely. For the poor face many of the same risks as the rest of society, such as illness, poor harvests, slow business cycles or death of income earners. However, because they are on the margin, with no insurance and little or no savings, they are in an even weaker position to deal with risks than the rest of society because a single illness could cost them everything (Krishna 2010; Roodman 2012). Despite all of this and the fact that the poor tend to be poorly educated, they are generally well aware of their finances and often manage them rather astutely (Collins et al. 2009).

## THE MAJOR PLAYERS

There are three major players in the functioning of microfinance that are the focus of this study. The first is the government. The government has the role of choosing to regulate or not regulate the microfinance industry. Some governments, such as in Bolivia, take a relatively laissez-faire approach. The policies and regulations the Bolivian government has established have been designed with the MFI in mind and a desire to facilitate its operations by supporting its business model. This lowers operating costs for the MFI. Market competition, of which there is plenty in Bolivia, should drive the cost of borrowing down, thereby benefiting the borrower. While this may be the case, there are some downsides to loose regulation. The major MFIs in Bolivia work extensively with the local indigenous populations, the Quechua and Aymara, but because of loose regulations, most documentation is in Spanish, or even English, rather than the customer's native language (Bateman 2010). On the other end of the spectrum, states like Nicaragua and Brazil have taken a very different approach, imposing more restrictive regulations, such as interest rate caps or limiting the amounts and duration of loans in an effort to try and protect the borrower. Another important characteristic of the government, which has already been mentioned, is its capacity and desire, or lack thereof, to create a well-functioning bureaucracy. This might include police, courts, employees in government ministries or offices, and more. A bureaucracy may be ineffective or inefficient for a number of reasons, but in the end it does not matter whether it is because of limited state capacity, as we might expect of Guatemala or El Salvador, for their trenchant poverty, or due to a lack of political will, as evidenced by Venezuela or Brazil. The outcome is the same; it is difficult and cumbersome to get things done through legitimate government channels. The government also determines whether the state is at war, either internally or externally, and the nature of the state's economic and political relationships. All of which might affect the strength of the economy and the investment climate.

Second are MFIs. This is, perhaps, the most obvious player in the microfinance industry, especially if one assumes that there are plenty of poor people who need financial services and are discerning price takers, who are willing to take loans as long as they see a potential for profit. Under those assumptions it falls to the MFIs to determine how to structure their services to maximize profits, outreach or impact. Indeed, depending on the state, MFIs often have endless configurations of loan sizes, durations, installment structures, requirements for subsequent loans, group dynamics and more. Microfinance institutions take a variety of forms. At the most basic level are rotating savings and credit associations (ROSCAs). These are groups of people, usually neighbors, friends or villagers who independently organize to help each other save money and leverage the group's cumulative capital to offer loans. These are completely detached from government and formal financial organizations. They are also small and localized, control very small amounts of capital and can be fleeting.

NGOs often operate formal institutions that do many of the same things as ROSCAs, if in a slightly different way. NGOs typically run non-profit

MFIs that depend on subsidized funding, at least to get started, and sometimes simply to maintain operations, though most have the goal of achieving sustainability. Many NGO-based MFIs have achieved sustainability, but they also tend to be smaller than commercially funded MFIs. This category of MFI typically faces significant restrictions on the types of services they can offer their customers in most countries because they are not regulated by the same laws that regulate financial institutions. Non-profits are exempt from taxes in most states, which is financially beneficial, but also usually comes with regulations on what they can and cannot do. Another reason that non-profits are more restricted in the services they can offer is that they are not monitored as carefully as banks are. Therefore, the state limits the activities they are permitted to engage in to protect customers, and the institution itself in the case of financial mismanagement.

The next level up includes non-banking financial institutions. These are somewhat akin to payday lenders in the US. They are not technically banks, but they do a lot of the same things as banks. They tend to have a freer hand than NGOs in terms of the types of services they can offer their customers, but not always. Finally, commercial banks occasionally delve into the microfinance industry or, as has happened with several MFIs that started out as non-profit NGOs, they evolve to take on bank status. These institutions face all of the same types of regulations and oversights as other banks. They also tend to finance themselves through the same channels as other commercial banks, which affords them access to the same volumes of capital as other commercial banks. Most MFIs that accept deposits into savings accounts are formally banks. Some MFIs are public, rather than private. They are either established, or operated by governments. Government-controlled or -operated MFIs are generally either non-banking financial institutions (NBFIs) or banks.

The third actor whose decisions matter is the customer. Customers, I assume, are not mindless machines who will take loans at any price because their discount rate is so high. Rather, customers are generally cautious individuals who are aware of how saving and borrowing money affects them over the short and long terms (Collins et al. 2009). This makes sense when one realizes that the poor generally have access to micro-credit by borrowing money from loan sharks, but avoid doing so because it is so expensive. Formal MFIs provide an opportunity to make lump-sum purchases that can improve their quality of life, perhaps through income-generating activities, but which they would not be able to finance without access to a formal lender. The poor are not ignorant of business, but, in fact, are often entrepreneurs (Baker 2014).

The choices and actions of these three players are at the root of the structure of microfinance in countries around the world. More importantly for this study, the government and MFIs affect the poverty, or quality of life, of the customer. The MFI is regulated, or not, by the government and is generally designed to serve the poor. The customer is often the target audience for the regulations the government might impose on the microfinance sector, as well as the clientele and raison d'être of the MFI.

## HOW IT ALL FITS TOGETHER

It is important to analyze the behavior of the key actors, their motivations and decision making calculus. The first step is to discuss assumptions about the actors that are key to understanding how they behave. Then it is possible to explain why risk is key in microfinance decision making and how it shapes the actors involved. The final section details how all of this translates to the real world; what the relationships should look like and how they should function.

### Assumptions

It becomes useful to make a few simple assumptions about the actors. All actors are assumed to fit the patterns typical of economic theories. Microfinance customers are assumed to be rational decision making, utility maximizers. They understand that an action leads to an outcome with a certain degree of probability. They know the cost of a given action and their valuation of the outcome, but the probability of actually realizing that outcome presents an unknown. Therefore, individuals make decisions based on an expected utility, or the value of the outcome minus the cost of the action, and discounted according to the degree of uncertainty accorded by the probability of realizing the outcome. An actor, though rational, might not seek her most desired outcome, even when the cost of doing so is small, if the probability of the desired outcome is too low.

It also assumed that all actors involved have a reasonably accurate understanding of the effects of policies, political events and economic conditions. Individual customers are almost certainly uneducated in the formal study of economics, but it is not unreasonable to assume that they understand the ins and outs of the industry in which they work. For example, a factory worker understands that, depending on the industry, there might be busy times when income will be good, and there might be slow times when income will be poor. A farmer knows that income arrives when he sells his crops, and he may get a better price if he can wait for a while after the harvest when supply begins to wane before he sells his goods (Sen 1999). The street merchant understands that if the government implements a law that requires street vendors to have a permit of some sort it might be worth shirking on the permit and paying bribes to local officials that will allow him to continue vending. It is clear that the poor, like most members of the working class worldwide, are familiar with their industry and have a certain degree of understanding about how government policies, political events and economic conditions might affect their incomes.

## The Role of Risk

Risk is the key to understanding the concerns and motivations that drive the decisions of MFIs and their customers. It can come from a number of sources and plagues all parties to a greater or lesser degree. Consider first the MFI. Its purpose is to provide financial services to the poor. One of the key services upon which most focus a great deal of their attention is the provision of credit. Extending credit has always been a risky venture. The lender generally gathers as much information as possible about the borrower in order to determine the likelihood that the borrower will not be able to repay. On the other hand, the borrower also has to assess her risk. She must think about how to use a loan in the short-term and how much return she might receive from the loan, relative to how much the loan will cost.

### MFIs' Risk

The lender takes the probability of default into account when setting the terms of the loans, including the interest rate, when the loan is due and how often the borrower must make payments. This is the case for MFIs as well. Risk is inherent in giving loans because the lender cannot know for certain whether the borrower will repay the money. Lenders try to mitigate the effects of risk by charging higher interest rates to borrowers who seem less likely to repay the debt in full and on time. However, the lender also has to charge enough interest that the expected utility is positive. That is, the potential rewards for lending to a riskier borrower outweigh the possibility that the borrower might default on the loan.

This is often more difficult for MFIs to determine their portfolio risk than for banks because this information is rarely formally available on MFIs' clients. The states in which MFIs often operate are unlikely to have functioning credit bureaus that track an individual's credit history. So the MFI can't know whether a potential borrower has failed to repay past loans, or is already heavily indebted, thus making him unlikely to be able to repay an additional loan. To exacerbate the situation, the poor often work in the informal sector, so there are no official records of income. Therefore, the MFI cannot verify a customer's income and whether she is likely to be able to pay the agreed-upon installments. Traditional lenders also mitigate risk by holding some sort of collateral. Collateral might be in the form of a title to a vehicle or a deed to a house. But, again, with MFIs this is not generally an option since the poor have very little of value, and what they do have may not be a formally owned, transferable property (Woodruff 2001; de Soto 2000).

The key to microfinance's success is finding innovative ways to work around these problems. They often get around the lack of information about credit history and ability to repay loans by using a group lending mechanism. This puts the burden of selecting credit-worthy borrowers onto the social group. They have the information and it saves the lender from having to expend significant resources trying to determine the credit-worthiness of each borrower. However, it also means that each borrower's collateral is her social network. The stakes are high for the borrowers when they use their social network for collateral and the return is low for the lender when they rely on the social network for collateral since they cannot liquidate social networks and turn them into cash. Nonetheless, we know from past research that repayment rates tend to be quite high when this approach is used, especially considering how little a lender might know about the borrowers (Aghion and Morduch 2005). What the MFI cannot know, however, is whether or how much it actually costs borrowers to rely on their social networks for loan collateral if they found themselves unable to repay.[1] Group lending also helps overcome the lack of collateral problem, especially when coupled with lending schemes that allow for increasingly larger and more favorable loans. Then the other members of the group often have an incentive to repay a loan, even pressuring a shirking member or covering his payments if necessary, in order to secure future loans. Forced savings are yet another solution MFIs have devised to ensure that customers have incentives to repay their loans.

Despite these and other mechanisms MFIs have developed and implemented to counter uncertainty, they cannot eliminate it. None of these mechanisms is foolproof. Moreover, there is yet another source of uncertainty against which there is little an MFI can do to insulate itself. That is the uncertainty of future conditions. The MFI cannot know whether the economy will fall into recession and make loan repayment impossible for its customers. It cannot foresee any number of possible future scenarios, such as the government instituting new policies that damage the microfinance industry.

For example, in Nicaragua in mid-2008 MFI clients began to complain of mistreatment by MFIs. The political climate lent itself to a polarization of the microfinance industry. On the one hand were the for-profit, commercial MFIs, and on the other were the non-profit, subsidy-dependent MFIs (Bedecarrats, Bastiaensen, and Doligez 2012). A combination of changes in trade balances and the domestic credit and debt market led to a genuine credit crisis. MFIs began using strong-arm tactics to try and recover loans from customers who did not have the means to pay. Recently elected president Daniel Ortega, from the leftist Sandinista party, gave a speech in which he encouraged protesters to rebel against the microfinance industry, calling them "loan sharks." The protesters eventually started the *No Pago*! ("I won't pay") campaign, which received overt government support in 2009–2010 and wiped out nearly a third of the industry's portfolio and clientele.

Some of these types of tumultuous events might be predicted as a possibility, but many are unforeseen. The microfinance industry has a limited ability to predict such events. However, they can monitor conditions that might spark such events. For example, the election of Daniel Ortega might have set off warning bells for some MFIs. As a former guerrilla fighter and the leader of a powerful new party that was changing the political power structures of the state, Ortega's response to strong-arming MFIs was not terribly surprising (Vanden and Prevost 2015). On the other hand, President Dilma Roussef of Brazil, who was elected in 2010, is also a former guerrilla fighter and from a leftist party which had made waves across Brazil. However, neither she nor her administration did anything that would suggest any hostility towards the microfinance industry in Brazil. Though to be fair, Brazil's microfinance industry is far more regulated than Nicaragua's was. Brazil has rather restrictive caps on interest rates and a significant portion of the microfinance industry is funded by the state. So the state has more control over the microfinance industry and the extreme conditions that prevailed during Nicaragua's credit crisis would likely have been avoided through state intervention in Brazil.[2]

These are all things that must be considered when investors contemplate putting money into an MFI in a given country. They examine the economic outlook for the state and try to determine whether the economy is, or will be, stable and whether micro-enterprises will be successful. They look at whether there exists a reliable credit bureau or similar institution, whether the legal system is mature enough that the MFI would be able to rely on courts to enforce contracts and whether the legal system acknowledges private property rights and such. All these concerns play into the calculus of the investor.

## *Borrowers' Risk*

Risk also generally influences the poor in their decisions whether to borrow or not and whether to repay or not. While some MFI clients might borrow money without regard for their ability to repay it in the future, most are well aware of their finances and what they are capable of (Dowla and Barua 2006; Collins et al. 2009). A poor person who is a potential customer for an MFI faces risk from multiple sources. First, there is a risk that stems from the inherent uncertainty surrounding the types of employment in which they often engage. Street vendors and shopkeepers have good days, when their goods sell well and they make a good profit, and bad days, when they make little or no profit. Another common employment in some countries is that of taxi driver, whether bicycle taxi, motorcycle taxi, or otherwise. These also experience good days and bad days, and good seasons and bad seasons. Farmers deal with the uncertainty that stems from the variability of weather conditions. Not enough rain and the crops wither, but too much and they drown or wash away. Or even the right amount of rain but at the wrong time can kill a crop or at least decrease harvest. Rain is just one variable, as there are also unexpected freezes, hailstorms, pests and so on.

All of these uncertainties create risk. There is a risk that the harvest will not be as large as expected, or that the taxi will need unanticipated repairs, or even that income earners will be unable to work for some reason. All of these are unknowns that the customers have to consider (Collins et al. 2009). A portion of this risk is passed on to the MFI as well, since the customer might be unable to repay loans. Fortunately, some MFIs have become quite adept at creating products that account for these uncertainties and allow some flexibility in repayment schedules and lending terms that allow customers to repay when they are able. Unfortunately, these are not common practices because it reduces returns or ties up capital, shifting uncertainty to the MFI and limiting its potential profitability (Dowla and Barua 2006).

Like MFIs, the poor also face uncertainties at the state level. Poor economic conditions caused by bad governance or simply unfavorable policies to their industry could drive down incomes. Many of the poor and near-poor work in factories in some countries. Often these factories export their products overseas, which means they are subject to the political-economic relationships of the states involved. A souring of relations could mean the factory decreases production and lays off workers, or at least decreases hours. A general slowing of economic growth among trade partners could have the same effect. Moreover, poor countries are far more likely than wealthier, more stable states to be subject to intrastate conflicts or other political instability that might upset the economic lives of citizens in the country (Collier 2007).

It has often been stated in the context of Latin American politics and economies that when the US sneezes, Latin America comes down with the flu (Skidmore, Smith, and Green 2014). When the US decided to subsidize corn ethanol in the mid-2000s in order to push for green alternatives to fossil fuels, it drove up corn prices. The jump in corn prices looked like ripples in the US, but more closely resembled shockwaves in much of Latin America where millions of people live on the margin. The jump in corn prices made access to basic food more expensive. It also drove up prices on most kinds of meat, since commercial livestock are fed corn as a staple of their diets. This was in part what led to the economic problems in Nicaragua mentioned previously and led to the *No Pago* campaign. These state-level interactions can have large, unanticipated impacts at the household level.

Another source of risk for borrowers in many poor states comes from the functioning of the bureaucracy. Entrepreneurs are often obliged to pay bribes in order to get licenses or permits, or to avoid even greater fines (Hunt and Laszlo 2012). The poor might also violate ordinances that are only rarely or weakly enforced in order to increase their profits, but doing so generally involves the risk of being punished for the violation. A very notorious example of this was when a young man in Tunisia was selling produce on the side of the road and government officials confiscated his vegetable cart, saying that he did not have the proper permits. When he went to the local government administration building he was turned away and told he could not get his vegetables or cart back. The young man, already living on the margin and in despair of being able to survive, doused himself in gasoline and self-immolated in front of the government office building. This action led to protests that sparked the Arab Spring, civil wars and the fall of several regimes.

In addition to corruption and its inefficiencies is the question of state capacity. In many of the poorest states the government is not always able to enforce the rule of law all of the time. Collins et al. (2009) recount a story about a rickshaw taxi driver who worked for another person who owned the rickshaw taxis he drove. The driver received from an MFI a loan large enough to buy a new rickshaw, which he suggested to interviewers would increase his profits by as much as 50%. He did not buy his own taxi, though, because he had nowhere safe to keep it overnight and was afraid that it would be vandalized or stolen during the night. The state's inability to enforce the rule of law was costing him a great deal of lost income.

For many families living on the edge of poverty, a single illness could be the difference between a stable, if modest, lifestyle and abject poverty (Krishna 2010). If an income earner is incapacitated by malaria or dengue fever for a couple of weeks, the lack of income could mean that the family has to borrow money, whether from an MFI or a loan shark, that it cannot afford to repay in order to eat. Barring that, it may have to sell essential possessions that it will need to reacquire at some point in the future. Even a child who becomes ill requires medical attention, which has associated costs including doctor's visits, medication, and a caretaker. In fact, one study reports that as much as one third of people living in poverty in some countries were not born into poverty but fell into it through a series of unfortunate events (Thapa 2010). The death of an income earner could have the same effect as a major illness in a family (Collins et al. 2009; Roodman 2012). These same risks exist in developed countries, but the families in those countries have the benefit of Social Security benefits to a deceased income earner's dependents, health insurance, and legislation that protects an income earner if she needs to address medical needs for herself or a family member.

Risk and uncertainty is inherent in life, whether a person is rich or poor. The difference lies in the ability to manage risk. An average middle-class American has an insurance policy to cover nearly every aspect of life—auto, home, life, health, perhaps disability, or other types of insurance. She also has access to a number of financial services that can be used as informal insurance, such as credit cards for when unforeseen costs arise. Home equity lines of credit or personal loans can be used to cover major expenses, like life cycle events (i.e. weddings, funerals, etc.). The poor, on the other hand, rarely have access to, or can afford, formal insurance. Nor do they always have access to the variety of legitimate financial services that middle-class Americans do. This leaves them fully exposed to the raw, impoverishing effects of unemployment, illness and death. Even in the case of personal loans, a borrower in a developed country can file for bankruptcy protection if she runs into severe financial hardship, as mentioned in the previous chapter. The poor in developing countries have no such security.

## BUILDING THE THEORETICAL MODEL

Answering the research questions posed in the first chapter requires one to think about microfinance at the individual and the state levels. First, a customer must decide for him- or herself whether to deposit savings, take out a loan or buy insurance with a MFI. Assuming that these individuals are rational actors, they will take advantage of the services offered by MFIs only if they believe it is in their own best interest. Since MFIs generally direct their services to the poor, the customers' interests should be easy to deduce. Accepting Maslow's hierarchy of needs as universally applicable, and taking what we know of the poor in developing countries, those individuals are struggling to secure their most basic needs, the physiological needs and safety needs (Maslow 1943). Their behavior should be very predictable; they will do whatever they think is going to secure those needs. In fact, Collins et al. document this struggle in *Portfolios of the Poor* (2009). The families they followed over the course of a year often went to great lengths to borrow money when necessary to ensure that their basic needs were met.

Many studies have tried to understand how microfinance affects poverty and have arrived at a variety of different conclusions. Some, like David Roodman (2012), find no significant impact on poverty in randomized controlled trials (Dean, Karlan, and Zinman 2011; Duvendack et al. 2011), but others are optimistic and find that microfinance improves the quality of life of customers on a number of different measures (Brau and Woller 2004; Ahlin, Jiang, and Paper 2005; Latifee 2012; Odell 2011). The nearly universal problem, though, is that it does not make sense to think about how microfinance affects poverty in isolation; governmental policies and regulations must be considered as well. Indeed, many researchers have addressed the relevance of the state (Duflos and Imboden 2003; North et al. 2008), though few have looked, specifically, at how the state might affect the impact that microfinance might have on the poor.

There are two distinct but related effects a state can have. First, the government plays a role in policy making and regulation of the microfinance industry, which affects the sustainability and viability of microfinance. Many states limit the types of services that non-banking financial institutions can offer their customers. Some states try and prevent exploitation of the poor by imposing interest rate limits on MFIs, or requiring that the MFI take specific measures to help customers understand all of the costs associated with a loan. On the other end of the spectrum, some states subsidize and promote the microfinance industry, offering cheap capital, preferential credit terms, or even engaging directly in microfinance through state-run MFIs. Second, governance also affects the calculus and expectations of poor individuals who might take advantage of microfinance opportunities. The customer alone must determine whether a micro-loan will be of benefit when it is available. Her decision is likely influenced by how difficult it will be to set up or expand a microenterprise. Things like bureaucratic corruption, or how much foot traffic the city's infrastructure supports, might also affect it. So the effect of governance is felt at two different stages—first it affects the microfinance industry itself, and second, it affects whether the poor are able to benefit from microfinance. This focus on how the government might affect microfinance's impact on the poor is what makes this work unique.

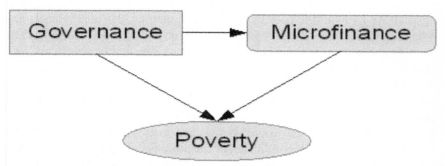

Figure 3.1.   Governance—Microfinance—Poverty Relationship

## Relationship 1

Although there is a great deal about economic development that scholars do not yet understand very well (North et al. 2008), there are some relationships that are generally accepted and over which the government of a state has some degree of control. First, government has some degree of influence over the macroeconomic stability of the national economy. Well-functioning states can use a number of tools to control inflation and money supply. A Keynesian approach to economics helps the government ameliorate the sting of recession by borrowing against periods of high growth. This smooths the sharp ridges and troughs out of the growth curve, making it easier to predict the future state of the economy with greater accuracy (Gilpin 1987; Rodrik and Wacziarg 2005). This makes it easier for investors and entrepreneurs to begin ventures because they can be more confident about future profit margins than in an economy prone to wide swings between growth and recession. Most governments also have some degree of control over interest rates, which has a direct impact on any MFI that has to borrow money in order to fund its loans and, by extension, affects the microfinance borrowers. Most governments also have some control over inflation, which affects spending and the money supply and will affect financial activity across the economy.

For example, in 1998 Brazilian officials had a difficult choice to make. The real was still a relatively new currency and its peg to the US dollar had helped stabilize runaway inflation just a few years before. However, economic pressure on the value of the real meant that policy makers had to choose whether to risk exhausting their foreign exchange reserves trying to hold the peg, and potentially having to devalue anyway, or devalue right away and allow the currency to float. Devaluing, they knew, would likely slow economic growth, at least for a year or two, reintroduce the possibility of runaway inflation, and potentially destabilize international trade (Vanden and Prevost 2015). They chose to devalue and move to a float, which made waves across the entire economy.

The second way the government controls the national economy is through its control of international trade, at least that which occurs in the formal market. International trade, while it may not have as direct an impact on microfinance as it does on FDI, for example, matters for the poor because when terms of trade are more favorable some industries grow while others do not. The industries in which the state has a comparative advantage should come to favor large firms and attract FDI and other industries will likely remain small and relatively insignificant (Barro 1997). Having a stable trade relationship also means that workers in the trade industry are more likely to have steady, or at least predictable, incomes (recall the corn ethanol example). Also, the spillovers of knowledge and technology often spur growth forward and make it easier for domestic firms to compete in the global market (Frieden and Kennedy 2006).

Third, governments can spend money on infrastructure to accommodate industrial growth. Although more important for some industries than others, a good infrastructure makes economic growth and stability much more likely (Collier 2007). The ability to transport labor to production facilities and goods to market, or to work continuously without interruption of electricity or other critical production inputs, is crucial for many industries. Ports, highways and electrical grids tend to be major selling points for investors because, again, they remove some of the uncertainty of business and allow them to predict success with greater accuracy.

Fourth, government can invest in human capital. Classical growth models suggest that expertise, or human capital, should be positively correlated with economic growth (Easterly 2001; Barro 1997). Although the data do not strongly support this connection (Easterly 2006), greater educational opportunities are an element of a higher standard of living since they open doors to more careers, not to mention increasing people's ability to understand and negotiate financial matters. For many people, education helps give meaning to life. Learning gives a sense of purpose.

Finally, implementing social safety net programs reduces poverty directly by offering food, housing, money or other resources to the poorest in a society. This increases the probability that basic physical needs are being met, and in so doing relieves a great deal of stress for those who would be at risk of falling deeper into poverty. There is the possibility that social safety nets create dependence, but whether dependent or not, those who benefit from social programs also experience less acute poverty. It creates a floor, below which nobody will fall. If a family experiences a catastrophe, they can rely on the social safety net, if it exists, to prevent them from suffering utter destitution.

*Hypothesis 1*

Regardless of the microfinance industry, governments with quality institutions will have lower poverty levels than governments with poor institutions.

Hypothesis 1a: States with greater economic stability will have less poverty

Hypothesis 1b: States with better international economic relations will have less poverty

Hypothesis 1c: States with better infrastructure will have less poverty

Hypothesis 1d: States with better educational opportunities will have less poverty

Hypothesis 1e: States with better social safety nets will have less poverty

## Relationship 2

Offering financial services to the poor will improve their standard of living if for no other reason than that it gives them options. Collins et al. (2009) tracked more than 250 households for a full year, interviewing them at least twice each month to find out as much as they could about their financial lives. It is difficult for people living in developed, industrialized states to imagine how households living on less than $2 a day per person could have money to manage, but it turns out that they are often involved in savings groups or self-help groups, such as ROSCAs, borrowing money from friends, family or neighbors and sometimes borrowing from informal moneylenders. The authors say, "Money management is, for the poor, a fundamental and well-understood part of everyday life" (page 3). Those who are able to do it well are much more likely to improve their quality of life compared to those who are not as adept. They also say they often found that "poor households are frustrated by the poor quality—above all the low reliability—of the instruments that they use to manage their meager incomes" (page 3). The implication is that a more reliable way to save, or a more consistent supply of credit, would reduce financial stress for these individuals.

Microfinance, whether it is heavily regulated or not, is a formal financial option for the poor, an option that they probably would not have without the locally operating MFI.[3] If an MFI opens a branch in a new village, the villagers may choose not to patronize the MFI if it is an inferior option to those they already use. However, if it is a better option, access to financial services through the MFI should make it easier to manage finances. Logic suggests that if a poor household is relying on being able to borrow money from friends and family when necessary, or has lent money and is relying on it being repaid when necessary, there will be a good deal of uncertainty with these interactions. As discussed before, one of the greatest challenges that the poor often face is the irregularity of incomes. A factory slowdown, a poor harvest, or a slow day at the market could mean little or no income for days or weeks. A formal financial institution may be able to help some households to add a degree of stability to their finances. Customers of those MFIs with inflexible repayment plans can take loans when they are needed and plan ahead to pay installments. This does not, by any means, eliminate the risks described earlier that the poor often face, but it provides them with a mechanism to help compensate for those risks. Some MFIs offer flexible repayment schedules to accommodate the irregularity of income that tends to plague the poor. The poor still get the loans when they need them, but can repay when they have income.

Of course, it is also possible that customers of those MFIs with inflexible payment schedules might not adequately plan ahead and find themselves subject to collectors with no ability to pay. Although MFIs may be shifting away from some of the brutal collection tactics that have been reported in the past, there is anecdotal evidence that some households have been left much worse off because they were unable to repay their loans or were forced to sell other possessions in order to do so (Roodman 2012). Moreover, it is possible for poor households to become over-indebted. Because there is generally little communication between MFIs, and often no effective credit monitoring mechanism, it is possible for MFI clients to borrow from several MFIs simultaneously—leading to over-indebtedness. Alternatively, a client might find herself unable to repay one loan so she takes a second to pay the first and a third to pay the second and so on into a debt spiral of financial ruin. This may be exacerbated by MFIs that push their loans or that do not facilitate borrowers' understanding of repayment terms and conditions. However, MFIs have incentives to avoid perpetuating debt cycles or over-indebtedness because it makes a customer considerably less likely to be able to repay her loan when the time comes, which would mean that the MFI gets stiffed. In addition to reducing profit from loans, exploitative business practices may also drive away investors since most MFIs around the world are closely monitored by a variety of ratings agencies. Moreover, abusive practices could spark a revolt, as occurred in Nicaragua in 2009–2010, heavily damaging local MFIs.

Loans are not the only services that MFIs offer, though. Perhaps one of the most important is savings services (Ahlin, Jiang, and Paper 2005; Dupas and Robinson 2010; Islam 2009; Barro 1997). To counteract the lack of restraint that most people tend to struggle with, poor households will sometimes ask other people to hold their savings for them, or else they lend it to somebody who needs it now, but agrees to repay before the owner will need it. The problem is that neither of these mechanisms is very reliable. Collins et al. (2009) reported, unsurprisingly, that loans were not repaid on time, or the person holding the money spent it. Moreover, a jar of money sitting on the mantel is more easily spent than is the money tucked safely away in a savings account that requires a waiting period for withdrawal. Whether because of family members with little self-restraint, or friends and neighbors wanting to borrow money, poor households often have trouble holding onto their savings. Having a formal savings mechanism would remove a great deal of the uncertainty and provide a balance against the lack of self-restraint most people suffer from. Admittedly, however, many MFIs are legally precluded from accepting deposits, and therefore are limited to micro-credit.

While there is room for microfinance to help people spin themselves ever deeper into debt, intuitively this should be the exception rather than the rule. If people regularly found themselves worse off from taking a microloan, they would not take any more loans and would almost certainly discourage others from taking loans. The borrower who found herself trapped in a debt cycle would serve as an example of the risks of borrowing to the rest of her social network. Therefore, if people are taking loans, this suggests that they must be receiving some benefit from doing so. Indeed, other lending and borrowing options likely persist, even with an MFI in the village, so the MFI simply provides the household with one more option. They will exercise that option only if they believe that it will meet their needs more effectively than the alternatives. All of this suggests the following hypothesis.

*Hypothesis 2*

Regardless of the quality of government institutions, more microfinance will lead to lower poverty levels.

While it seems intuitive that microfinance should help borrowers and only rarely leave a few worse off, as chapter 2 demonstrated, the literature is quite conflicted on this. Many experts have suggested that the beneficial effects of microfinance might be washed out by the harm MFIs do to some households (Karlan and Zinman 2009; Islam 2009). Many researchers, both in academia and those working in the private sector, have conducted innumerable impact studies to try and determine the precise effect of microfinance. In fact, guides have been written explaining all of the things a researcher should consider when conducting an impact study. As mentioned, however, the results have been mixed. The results from the empirical investigation in the next chapter will by no means constitute a conclusive declaration, but will add to the evidence and will provide a baseline against which to compare subsequent models that examine how microfinance is affected by the quality of institutions.

Clearly, though, when the government is properly regulating the microfinance industry and maintains appropriate, well-functioning institutions, the effect of microfinance should be more positive than otherwise. Where the rule of law is strictly enforced, for example, the rickshaw taxi driver from the anecdote above would not have to forgo buying his own rickshaw for fear that it would be vandalized or stolen. There are some specific institutions that might be particularly influential in making microfinance more effective. Some of the specific institutions that might matter because they affect risk and uncertainty include credit bureaus or similar institutions, effective law enforcement, and functioning courts.

The existence of credit bureaus is something that many people in industrialized states take for granted. In fact, in the United States there are three such credit bureaus which track individuals' credit histories and several others which track commercial entities' credit histories. An entire cottage industry has arisen around these institutions claiming to be able to help improve an individual's credit rating, or protecting credit ratings in the event of identity theft or other forms of fraud. For citizens of the developed world, credit scores matter. They affect your ability to buy a house or a car, or to get a credit card, and they are one of the key drivers in determining how much you will pay for the credit. In many developing states, there are no such institutions. Consequently, the lender has no background information it can use to determine how much money it is safe to lend and at what rate it should lend in order to cover opportunity costs and to account for the possibility that the borrower fails to repay the loan.

This, and the lack of collateral, is what has led MFIs to come up with innovative ways around these problems. Unfortunately, their solutions are not always ideal. For example, group lending models almost inherently require a certain rigidity in their repayment schedules since if the group were allowed to miss or delay payments, group members would have less incentive to pressure each other to make their individual contributions. Late payments by individuals and the group would spiral out of control and fall into a tragedy of the commons. The rigid schedules, though, do not allow an MFI to tailor a financial service to a specific customer's needs. Since the poor often struggle with inconsistent incomes, rigid repayment schedules reduce the utility of a micro-loan.

The lender is left with little choice but to assume the worst by charging interest rates high enough to account for the possibility of default. The problem may be exacerbated because the borrower would have no incentive to repay the loan since she could simply go to another lender the next time she needed money and her previous failure to pay would not affect her ability to secure a new loan. The uncertainty would almost necessarily lead to inefficiencies; either the lender charging too much, thus hurting the borrower, or charging too little, and hurting itself. If the lender manages to stay in business, though, we can assume that it has opted for the former, charging top interest rates in order to cover risk, otherwise the lender would go under. All of this could be avoided if the MFI knew more about the individual's financial history and had a mechanism for punishing customers who do not repay loans.

Other institutions, such as the rule of law, which might also be stated as a functioning, reliable, honest police force, likely augment the effect of microfinance. The rule of law and corruption both deal with predatory behavior that distorts the market and decreases efficiency and competitiveness (Hall and Jones 1999). The rule of law mitigates violence, ensures the security of the person and protects property rights through contract enforcement and efficient institutions. It also serves as an institutional check against government to counter the government's ability to renege on agreements, regulates private capture and limits corruption by ensuring equal treatment and avoiding rent-seeking behavior (Haggard and Tiede 2011). While some people engage in productive behavior, such as farming, others might engage in predatory behavior such as stealing the farmer's crops, or bureaucratic corruption by eliciting bribes to allow the farmer to sell his crops at the local market without appropriate permits or interference. The latter two produce nothing useful and, therefore, create a drag on society and on the economy. So the rule of law should help reduce at least a portion of predatory behavior, and thereby reduce the portion of otherwise productive labor devoted to guarding against thieves and such. Likewise, corruption reduces the farmer's net income since bribes must be paid from what would otherwise be profits (Mauro 1995; Murphy, Shleifer, and Vishny 1991).

The legitimate functioning of each of these institutions should increase the poverty reduction effectiveness of microfinance. Each institution has a direct effect on the entities involved in microfinance and their proper functioning would decrease uncertainty and risk, thus making the relationships more efficient and profitable. However, it is not only the existence of certain institutions that matters. Certain characteristics of these and other institutions, indeed the functioning of the bureaucracy as a whole, will determine its ability to facilitate and even promote stable and efficient outcomes, which will likely impact microfinance.

An important characteristic of the political system is its degree of stability. Political and economic stability are intimately related since the government plays a major role in promoting economic stability and economic stability often plays a major role in promoting satisfaction with the government and, therefore, its longevity. Economic stability includes a whole host of variables, from the stability of the currency to the stability of interest rates, exchange rates, tax rates, and so on. It also includes the degree of variation in economic growth rates. All of these factors matter because of their effects on risk and uncertainty. For example, the more interest rates or inflation vary, the less confident a micro-entrepreneur or a household can be that it is either getting a better rate now than it could if it waited a few months, or that an investment now will be an asset rather than a liability in a few months or years.

As an example of economic instability changing investing patterns, many Americans considered real estate to be a safe investment prior to the great recession. Homeowners in Las Vegas saw home prices climb steadily beginning in the late 1990s. Average prices climbed from 84% of average income in 1999 to surpass 100% by mid-2002 ("US House Prices: Reality Check" 2014).[4] Prices reached 140% just two years later and peaked in 2005 at nearly 170% of average income. Up to the peak, investors were betting big on real estate. People were buying houses they could ill afford because the nearly decade-long trend had been consistently and rapidly increasing home values. Unfortunately for many homeowners, the rapid growth created an asset bubble in the market, and when the bubble popped, real estate prices went into a near freefall. The decline in house prices was just as steep as the increase, but it did not bottom out until 2011, when average house prices dropped below 70% of average incomes. For those who bought at the top of the bubble and had to sell at the bottom, the consequences were devastating. It led to an epidemic of foreclosures as homeowners went upside-down on their mortgages, owing thousands of dollars more than the market value of the house. Some people lost their down payment, years' worth of mortgage payments, and their credit score when the economic instability forced them into a short sale or foreclosure.

This particular episode of economic instability affected far more than just the housing market. The financial sector, which held most of the mortgages that homeowners began defaulting on in 2006, also went into a tailspin which froze credit markets for several quarters. GDP growth dropped to near zero, poverty spiked, home ownership rates dropped and unemployment jumped. The instability of the market made houses that had been assets into liabilities that severely damaged many families. Governments try to avoid this kind of instability because of the damage it causes for voters and for the economy at large.

Economic stability is the justification for all kinds of economic manipulation by governments around the world. They overspend during recessions, knowing they will have to underspend later to compensate, in effect borrowing from tomorrow's economic growth to ease today's recession (Heilbroner 1953). It is one of the key reasons governments manipulate monetary policy, because deflation and excessive inflation are both extremely damaging to the economy. It was the reason for the provision of a gold standard and the IMF under the Bretton Woods system after World War II and for the creation of the Eurozone within the European Union. It is all done for the sake of economic stability. The more certain an actor can be of future profits, the more efficiently she can maximize her investment portfolio today. Governments play a major role in promoting, even creating, economic stability, and economic stability plays a major role in individual or household-level financial decisions.

In an effort to stabilize the economy, the United States launched a massive stimulus plan in 2008 to try and address the recession. The government expended far more than its revenue in an attempt to encourage economic growth. It re-capitalized banks in order to loosen up credit markets and manufacturers in order to save jobs. It subsidized housing costs for some individuals and expanded the social safety net for millions. All of this was done in the name of stability and feeding growth. However, it jumped the national debt from less than $8 trillion in 2005 to more than $16 trillion by 2013, despite bitter complaints and dire warnings of economic meltdown coming from some groups within the US.

Stability is also important because it serves as the primary indicator of future conditions. If the political system remains stable, our proverbial farmer knows more or less what to expect in terms of the costs of production and the values or prices paid for certain goods, all else being equal. If the government is unstable, on the other hand, the farmer's uncertainty about the future will act as a deterrent against behavior with any associated risk. A civil war, which is a much higher risk in developing countries, or other equally disturbing event has obvious and direct effects at the household level. Without addressing the very real human costs, when young men and women take up arms it comes with an opportunity cost. Those involved in the fighting could be producing things that improve people's quality of life. Each time a fighter is killed a bit of human capital is destroyed. Manufacturing facilities and infrastructure are often prime targets for attacks, which deteriorates the economy's productive capacity and efficiency.

However, less severe events can also impact the household. In 2014, peaceful protests in Hong Kong froze up transportation networks, making it difficult or impossible for people to get to work. This relatively mild incident may have cost the city's retailers more than a quarter of a billion dollars (BBC News 2014). The prevalence and audacity of drug cartels in Mexico were escalating throughout the 2000s, and by the end of the first decade, beheadings and open gun battles in the streets were somewhat common. Normal citizens felt endangered and began fleeing towns where the cartels were most prolific (Burnett 2010). When Hugo Chávez took office in Venezuela and ratified the new constitution, it had significant impacts on the political system and on the people. The economy contracted 5% his first year in office. One of his political objectives was to spread the oil wealth among a larger segment of the population. He fired the oil company's president in early 2002, which led to protests, a short-lived coup d'etat, 30% inflation, 20% unemployment and a 13% drop in economic productivity for the year (Skidmore, Smith, and Green 2014).

Potential microfinance customers or microentrepreneurs should be more hesitant to start a microenterprise if they are uncertain whether they will be able to turn a profit and repay their loan on time if the business climate should sour (Islam 2009). What might be a safe business venture in a stable economy becomes a risk with potentially large losses, and probably no greater profits, in an unstable or unpredictable economy. The expected utility, based on the probability of success and the likely payoffs from either outcome, quickly shrinks to zero or goes into the negative when uncertainty increases risk (Driver et al. 2004; Most and Starr 1989).

In traditional finance and investment, investors only make risky investments if the payoff is large enough to balance the risk. At the same time, both theory and history have shown that investing too much in a risky venture can be devastating (Ferguson 2009). Wise investors prefer, instead, to diversify their portfolios; they put some money in sure-fire investments with low returns, and some in higher risk investments that might be high yield if the investment is successful. For micro-credit borrowers, however, the loans offered to them often represent large investments relative to their regular income. Since the poor, by definition, do not have other large investments, they have a lot riding on their ability to successfully improve their standard of living with the loans they take. Theory and history both suggest that they should be very sensitive to risk (Ferguson 2009). It seems reasonable to assume that they have good information about risk since they are presumably investing in a venture with which they are already familiar or even already involved (Aghion and Morduch 2005). Our farmer should have a pretty good idea of the types of political or economic instability that are likely to affect the market.

General economic theory has been making these connections for several years (Easterly 2001, 2006; Haggard and Tiede 2011; Murphy, Shleifer, and Vishny 1991). Although there are only a few examples of researchers making this connection in the microfinance literature (*see* Ault and Spicer 2009 *as an example*), the FDI literature has clearly established the empirical link between the quality of government institutions and investment, both in terms of its prevalence and its success (Driver et al. 2004; Daude and Stein 2007). An uncertain market is typically not one that attracts investment because investors find it more difficult to predict their expected utility. That is to say, with any investment there is a risk of loss. Generally the return on the investment, call it a payoff, must be high enough that an investor is willing to take the risk, which might also be called the possibility of failure. A safe bet, such as a US treasury bill, which carries virtually zero risk, pays little interest so the payoff is small (Ferguson 2009). On the other hand, investing in a start-up technology company is quite risky, but the potential payoff is also quite large. When the market experiences high uncertainty it is, by definition, difficult to calculate the risk. In terms familiar to quantitative scholars, risk is a point estimate while uncertainty is a confidence interval. Political instability might both cause the confidence interval to expand and change the point estimate of the risk, although it is impossible to know by how much since the confidence interval is even larger than normal. Stated another way, when there is little instability an investor knows what he does not know, risk, but when uncertainty is high, the investor cannot be sure about what he does not know. Uncertainty generally compels investors to delay investment while they gather additional information (Cukierman 1980). This is especially true for poorer individuals who might be risking a great deal when they take a loan from an MFI (Binswanger 1980). I expect microfinance to be no exception.

*Hypothesis 3*

The higher the quality of governmental institutions, the greater the poverty reduction effect of microfinance.

Hypothesis 3a: The existence of a credit bureau should increase the poverty reduction effect of microfinance
Hypothesis 3b: The better the rule of law is in a country, the more effective microfinance should be for poverty reduction
Hypothesis 3c: States with greater political stability should see more poverty reduction from microfinance than less stable states
Hypothesis 3d: States with greater economic stability should see more poverty reduction from microfinance than less stable states

## CONCLUSION

In chapter 1 I raised a research question; how might a government affect whether and how much microfinance reduces poverty? This chapter discussed the mechanisms by which governments could be influencing the microfinance industry and how it influences the lives of the poor. Risk and uncertainty are key to understanding these relationships. They are an integral part of any rational investment decision, whether made by a bank or non-banking financial institution (NBFI), an enterprise, or a household. All must ask themselves, "what if the worst should happen?" The response to such a question, along with its associated probability and the expected utility of the investment, colors the investor's willingness and expectations. I make the case that greater certainty leads to more efficient investments while uncertainty makes investment unattractive.

The key point made in this chapter, though, is that governments can have a major impact on uncertainty and risk. The quality and functioning of institutions such as credit bureaus, police forces and legitimate courts decrease risk. Likewise, the institutional characteristics within the state matter too. Such characteristics as legal origin and political or economic stability can change the risk calculus as well.

## NOTES

1. Among the lower income categories in most developing countries, a much higher percentage of households are headed by single women when compared to the general population (Baker 2014). Men who are in the bottom socioeconomic categories tend to be mobile. Their mobility means that they typically have fewer social connections and rely less on their social network.

2. Another potentially significant difference between Ortega and Rousseff was that Ortega's party was relatively new, or at least, new again, to the Nicaraguan political landscape. Rousseff, on the other hand, was the successor to the real power figure behind her Workers' Party—Luiz Inácio "Lula" da Silva. Although the microfinance industry began to grow rather quickly under Cardoso, before Lula took office, Lula's economic policies were relatively conservative (see chapter 4). Policies began to change only gradually and in an otherwise relatively stable political and economic environment.

3. In fact, many poor still do not have access to MFIs or their services, either because no MFI has established a branch in their village, or because of constructed social limitations (Aghion and Morduch 2005).

4. All housing data are from economist.com, which gathered housing and income data from Standard & Poor's, Core Logic and Moody's Analytics. The measure used here compares average home prices against median income for major cities.

*Chapter Four*

# Looking at the Data

In the case of microfinance, it seems very likely that the quality of governance at the state level and the institutions and conditions within which the MFIs must operate influence the intended outcomes of microfinance. This might include the possibility of political instability, fluctuations in the value of currency or trade relations, the effectiveness and reliability of the court system and more. If this is true, we should be able to observe some differences among states in their progress towards poverty alleviation. I find mixed results, however, for the types of factors that seem to affect microfinance effectiveness as well as the magnitude of this effect. Some hypotheses are supported by the empirical evidence while others are not.

## OPERATIONALIZING MICROFINANCE, GOVERNANCE AND POVERTY

Before we jump into testing hypotheses, we need to add a little more focus to the main concepts. Being clear about the key concepts and what, precisely, is meant by microfinance or governance will help the reader assess whether the empirical tests are good tests of the hypotheses, what the limits of the empirical tests might be, and what kinds of conclusions can reasonably be drawn from the empirical tests. Describing how the concepts are empirically measured will make more sense after clearly defining the terms. This also helps ensure that the theory is driving the empirical tests and not the other way around.

## Microfinance

The main element of the theory detailed in chapter 3 is the concept of microfinance. Accurately measuring microfinance requires some thought because there are a number of indicators that capture different aspects of microfinance. Many past studies, when they discuss microfinance, focus on the strength of the industry. Scholars have looked at the profitability of individual MFIs and of the industry as a whole, MFI durability, loan repayment information, and much more (Brau, Hiatt, and Woodworth 2009; Aghion and Morduch 2005; Schicks 2007; Ault and Spicer 2009). However, the relationships described in the previous chapter are clearly focused on the individual-level effects experienced by the microfinance customers. Therefore, past studies that focus on characteristics of the industry, or even institutions, have little to say about the impacts on incentives for individuals who participate in microfinance. The focus here is on the individuals rather than the institutions or the industry as a whole.

The key to this conception of microfinance is whether or not individuals who want loans are able to get them. This is sometimes called market saturation (Odell 2011). In a saturated market, anybody who wants to get a loan and can be trusted to repay it, should be able to get one. The poor are not limited by the number or location of MFI branches, nor by a shortage of capital within the industry. Very few markets have reached the point of saturation. For most countries there are still people who might like to access microfinance, but are unable to do so because it is not available to them.

A measure needs to be established that captures, if not the precise probability that an individual will be able to obtain a loan when she needs it, then an approximation of that data. Getting the perfect data would require an extremely extensive survey of not only microfinance customers, but also non-customers who might or might not have desired a loan at some time. Such an undertaking would be useful, but is beyond the scope of the current project. Additionally, it might not actually provide all that much greater accuracy beyond the measure devised here, especially considering the cost of such an endeavor. I approximate this data by examining the number of borrowers within the microfinance industry as a percentage of the total population of each country in each year. This focuses on micro-loans to the exclusion of other financial services, but since loans make up the lion's share of microfinance, and because the key economic principles which suggest connections between microfinance and poverty alleviation rely on the role of capital for investment, this is a reasonable measure. This provides an approximate indicator of how easy or difficult it is to get a micro-loan.

Admittedly, there are problems that make this measure less than ideal. For example, many customers, depending on the MFI and the country, might take and repay multiple loans in a given year, possibly from multiple MFIs. That is not captured by this measure. It also does not directly measure the number of people who would like to get a loan, but are unable to do so. On the other hand, it is a useful measure because it provides an indication of how extensive the microfinance industry is. Where the industry is tenuous, few loans will be offered to fewer customers, and the number of borrowers per population will be low. A country where relatively more people are able to secure loans indicates that loans are relatively easier to get. Therefore, this measure approximates the desired information.

Data on the number of borrowers comes from one of the primary sources of data on microfinance; the Microfinance Information Exchange (MIX). The MIX collects extensive data on microfinance institutions from around the world. Most of the data is self-reported, and much of it is independently verified for accuracy. It is widely regarded as valid and commonly used in microfinance research (Aghion and Morduch 2005; Ault and Spicer 2009; Morduch 2010; Thapa 2010). If there is any bias in the data, it is likely only a slight under-representation of small MFIs (Demirgüç-Kunt and Morduch 2011).

## Poverty

While poverty seems like a simple concept at first blush, measuring it turns out to be a bit complicated. The first hurdle any measure of poverty must address is which poverty line to adopt. For example, the national poverty line in a developed state, such as the US, is far different from the poverty level in an under-developed state, say one in sub-Saharan Africa. Some scholars and organizations rely on global poverty lines of perhaps $1/day per person, or $1.25 or $2. Others rely on official national poverty lines. The key to financial measures of poverty is to account for the cost of living in a given country (*see* Brau et al. 2009; *or* Imai, Gaiha, Thapa, and Annim 2012 *for a thorough discussion of poverty measures*).

After solving how to account for the varying cost of living around the world, the next challenge is to address the depth of poverty. Having a large population slightly below the chosen poverty line who struggle to make ends meet, but in the end only occasionally have to skip meals or delay seeking medical help when needed is probably not the same as having a large population far below the same poverty line. Those far below the poverty line will likely miss far more meals, and might never be able to seek qualified medical assistance when needed. Poverty has at least two dimensions: breadth and depth. Measuring either one is complicated by the tendency for poor in most developing economies to engage heavily in the informal grey market, where transactions are not tracked or reported. Capturing one of these dimensions precisely is difficult enough, but capturing both is a herculean task.

As an alternative, some scholars choose to use non-financial measures of poverty such as caloric intake, or consumption (Carmignani 2011). These have the advantage of tapping into the root of poverty, the scarcity of resources. Unfortunately, caloric intake and consumption are not very easy to measure and are indicators that people have only recently begun collecting. Scholars have devised a clever solution, though (Girod 2011). Infant mortality is directly affected by all aspects of poverty. People living slightly below the poverty line have higher-than-normal infant mortality rates, and infant mortality rates for those who are far below the poverty line are higher still. Moreover, infant mortality rates are much easier to track than income-based measures of poverty or caloric intake.

However, raw infant mortality figures vary widely across states from as low as two or three infant deaths per thousand live births in places like Japan, Sweden or Singapore and as high as 187 in Afghanistan. Infant mortality rates have some basis in history, culture, infrastructure, and so on, so raw measures of infant mortality might not accurately capture the concept of poverty described above. In fact, it is the change in infant mortality caused by government and microfinance that is of interest here, rather than the raw level of infant mortality. Consequently, the dependent variable is infant mortality in $t_0$ minus infant mortality in $t_1$, or the difference in the infant mortality rate from last year to this year. A positive coefficient indicates that the infant mortality increased and a negative coefficient indicates that it decreased.

## Governance

The multi-faceted nature of government, and especially the quality of governance, means that capturing this concept in a single indicator, or even a handful of indicators, is rather difficult. Indeed, chapter three suggested that there are some specific elements of governance that might have particular types of impacts on microfinance and poverty alleviation. Those specific elements of governance will each be dealt with individually as they come up.

The theory developed in the previous chapter suggests a relatively complex set of results. There are three relationships that it addresses and for which it generated testable hypotheses. The first relationship is between government and poverty, the second is between microfinance and poverty. The third relationship is the joint relationship of government and microfinance on poverty. Each relationship and each hypothesis is tested and results are discussed in turn.

## HYPOTHESIS 1: QUALITY INSTITUTIONS
## REDUCE POVERTY

The first hypothesis is that quality institutions should reduce poverty regardless of microfinance. This is well established in the literature, but is a key part of the theory driving this analysis. Testing this relationship empirically provides a baseline for the rest of the analysis. It also serves as a robustness check on the data that is used to test the other hypotheses.

The key explanatory variables have all been explained but there are other important concepts whose operationalizations deserve discussion. Beginning with sub-hypothesis *1a, states with greater economic stability will have less poverty*, the theory focuses on the stability of the macroeconomy, and particularly stable growth, as well as how this translates for individuals. Economic stability is captured using two indicators, inflation of consumer prices and GDP per capita growth. Economic performance is an indicator of the state's ability to craft and implement policies that keep the economy healthy. Two more indicators are used to create the main independent variable used to test sub-hypothesis *1b, states with better international economic relations will have less poverty*; they are international trade, both imports and exports, and FDI flows. For sub-hypothesis *1c, states with better infrastructure should have less poverty*, the percentage of the population with access to improved sanitation facilities and improved water sources is used to capture the quality of infrastructure in the state.

I use factor analysis to consolidate from several indicators down to a single measure for each. The logic behind factor analysis is that there is a latent variable that causes the indicators that are directly measured. From the data on the indicators it is possible to get an idea of what the latent variable driving the indicators looks like (Agresti and Finlay 1997). It is then possible to test the concepts against one another without getting lost in how one indicator might affect another indicator because the model reverse engineers the latent variable based on the observed indicators (Long 1983). Factor loadings indicate how influential the indicator was for reverse engineering the latent variable. In other words, the loadings display the weight of each element for the prediction of the latent variable. Uniqueness is the variance that is unique to that particular indicator. Generally, the greater the uniqueness, the lower the factor loading. Factor loadings are shown in table 4.1.

The ratio of female to male primary enrollment serves as a proxy for the availability of educational opportunities and investment in human capital for sub-hypothesis *1d, states with better educational opportunities will have less poverty*. Female to male primary enrollment is a good indicator of human

**Table 4.1. Factor Loadings and Uniqueness**

| | Infrastructure | Economic Stability | Economic Relations |
|---|---|---|---|
| Improved Sanitation Facilities | 0.786 | | |
| | 0.383 | | |
| Improved Water Source | 0.786 | | |
| | 0.383 | | |
| Risk for Exchange Rate | | 0.807 | |
| | | 0.350 | |
| Risk for GDP Growth | | 0.773 | |
| | | 0.402 | |
| Risk for Inflation | | 0.647 | |
| | | 0.582 | |
| Risk for Per Capita GDP | | −0.343 | |
| | | 0.883 | |
| Imports | | | 0.986 |
| | | | 0.028 |
| Exports | | | 0.982 |
| | | | 0.037 |
| FDI | | | 0.764 |
| | | | 0.416 |

*Note:* Factor loadings above and uniqueness below.

capital investment because it is indicative of the priority the state places on education. Since men are considered the primary income earners in many societies, their education is usually prioritized over women's education. So young girls are less likely to enroll in or complete school. A low ratio usually also means that only the elites, and perhaps some of the middle class, can afford to send their girls to school.[1]

Finally, public health expenditures as a share of total healthcare costs are proxies for the extent of social safety nets in a state; *1e, states with better social safety nets will have less poverty*. Healthcare can be quite expensive, and beyond the reach of many poor households. Where government spending on healthcare accounts for a large share of total healthcare spending it is indicative of pro-poor policies within the state. All of these data come directly from the World Bank or the Penn World Tables (Heston, Summers, and Aten 2012).

Table 4.1 shows factor loadings and uniqueness. It is clear from table 4.1 that the *Infrastructure* and *Economic Relations* factors both target in a tight pattern. *Economic Performance* is not quite as tightly grouped, but still fairly close. Table 4.2 displays regression results for tests of Hypothesis 1. The empirical analysis generally supports the hypothesis.

Column 1 presents the results for the *Economic Performance* factor. Since the data are panel data, with panels that may be correlated, a simple linear

**Table 4.2. The Effects of Institutions on Poverty**

| Change in Infant Mortality | (1) Panel Corrected S.E.s | (2) Panel Corrected S.E.s | (3) Two-Stage Least Squares | (4) Panel Corrected S.E.s | (5) Panel Corrected S.E.s |
|---|---|---|---|---|---|
| Economic Stability | -0.0589** (0.0225) | | | | |
| Economic Relations | | -0.109*** (0.0164) | | | |
| Infrastructure | | | -0.785* (0.324) | | |
| Health expenditure, public (% of total health expenditure) | | | | 0.00462 (0.00109) | |
| Ratio of female to male primary enrollment (%) | | | | | 0.0137 (0.00652) |
| GDP per capita (constant 2000 US$) | 0.0000266** (0.00000903) | 0.0000540*** (0.00000905) | 0.000136** (0.0000479) | | |
| Mortality rate, infant (per 1,000 live births) | -0.0338*** (0.00218) | -0.0326*** (0.00194) | -0.0638*** (0.0123) | | |
| Constant | -0.211* (0.0941) | -0.368*** (0.0793) | 0.238 (0.226) | -1.278*** (0.0815) | -2.385*** (0.653) |
| Observations | 358 | 373 | 385 | 318 | 319 |
| $R^2$ | 0.612 | 0.672 | 0.251 | 0.014 | 0.007 |

Standard errors in parentheses
* $p < 0.05$, ** $p < 0.01$, *** $p < 0.001$

regression would suffer from bias. Using panel corrected standard errors accounts for the possible bias by assuming and correcting for autoregression (Beck and Katz 1995). The model also includes two control variables, *GDP/capita* to account for the effect income levels almost certainly have on changes in infant mortality, and the *Infant Mortality Rate* because the lower the rate is the more difficult it becomes to achieve further reduction. *Economic Performance* is a statistically significant predictor of changes in the infant mortality rate. However, its substantive impact is relatively small. This model predicts that increasing *Economic Performance* from its 25th percentile to its 75th percentile will decrease the infant mortality rate by less than .1 deaths per 1,000 live births. This would be akin to shifting from Honduras in 1988, in the midst of the war on the contras in neighboring Nicaragua, and suddenly becoming Chile in 2011. This kind of change in economic performance is not easily or quickly achieved. The effect of this shift on poverty is clear and statistically significant, though modest.

*Economic Relations* is similarly statistically significant and with a similarly marginal substantive impact. The same change in *Economic Relations*, from the 25th percentile to the 75th percentile, yields a decrease in the infant mortality rate about ⅓ the size of the decrease for *Economic Performance*, at only about .036 fewer infant deaths per 1,000 live births. Again, this is a pretty considerable improvement in economic interactions. Peru was at about the 25th percentile in 1990, when it was still adjusting to civilian rule from the military regime. The military regime was revolutionary and independent in international affairs. The regime created policies to end what it called the subordination of the state's economy to foreign interests (Skidmore, Smith, and Green 2014). It also nationalized the state oil company, IPC. The government transitioned to civilian control in 1980, but not without subtle, and sometimes not-so-subtle, military influence. In 1990 the state was beginning to implement more neoliberal economic policies, but only slowly. By 2010, however, Peru was at around the 75th percentile in *Economic Relations*. Fujimori's reign had ended and successive peaceful transitions of power between civilian governments had helped usher in an era of economic improvement with fairly stable economic policies, growth and interaction. So, it took Peru two decades to move from the low end of the spectrum to the high end, but the estimated impact on poverty alleviation is disappointingly small.

The remaining three models are not statistically significant in one-tailed tests. So, two of the five sub-hypotheses find clear, though marginal, support from the empirical analysis, while the other three do not. Interestingly, it is the two indicators that are most clearly tied to the economy that are statistically significant while the other, more societal variables are not statistically significant. The evidence at this point is not overwhelming, but it is at least suggestive that institutions, at least certain types, affect poverty. Next we shall look at the impact that microfinance has on poverty alleviation.

## HYPOTHESIS 2: MICROFINANCE HELPS ALLEVIATE POVERTY

The premise of microfinance is that it provides needed financial services to the poor. As discussed previously, there are a number of reasons why the poor might find it difficult to access financial services. If one accepts neoliberal economic theory, which prevails among most western economists, capital is a critical input for production, and if a producer doesn't have capital to invest in production she should borrow capital to invest in order to improve her productive capacity. Indeed, in developing countries, which are, almost by definition, capital poor, a capital investment should return large productivity increases. So, the thinking goes, poor people in developing countries could be more productive if they could invest in their productive capacity. Microloans are a way for them to do just that.

To contextualize this, a seamstress in Bangladesh, if she were to buy a sewing machine, could dramatically increase the amount of sewing she can accomplish compared to sewing by hand. She will be so much more productive that she could afford to repay a loan with interest, and still be better off, even in the short term. So, removing the barrier to financial services, especially loans, should help poor people in developing countries to invest and work their way out of poverty. Hypothesis 2 suggests that this relationship might be stronger under some conditions and weaker under others, but it should hold regardless of political institutions. Indeed, many scholars have suggested that microfinance reduces poverty, even under the worst political conditions (Dowla and Barua 2006; La Torre and Vento 2006). If this is true it would be unique in many ways. Other common poverty reduction techniques depend on the cooperation and smooth functioning of the government.

If this hypothesis is true, then microfinance should have a statistically significant effect on poverty under any and all circumstances. Therefore, it may not be necessary to develop an independent test of this hypothesis. Only if the tests for hypothesis 3 show that microfinance reduces poverty under all tested conditions, will it become necessary to develop further tests for hypothesis 2. However, if in testing hypothesis 3 the data show that microfinance does not alleviate poverty under even a single condition, it will disprove hypothesis 2. Consequently, it makes sense to first test hypothesis 3 before discussing hypothesis 2.

# HYPOTHESIS 3: BETTER INSTITUTIONS
## SHOULD INCREASE THE IMPACT OF MICROFINANCE

The next question is whether the quality of governance and institutions modifies the effect of microfinance for the poor. There are several possible responses to this hypothesis. It may be that microfinance always works, but that it has a larger impact on poverty under certain conditions. On the other hand, it may be that microfinance only affects poverty when conditions are just right. A third possibility is that microfinance is good for poverty under some conditions and bad for poverty under other conditions. Finally, it may be that microfinance never helps the poor under any conditions. Any of these findings would advance our understanding of this mechanism.

## Credit Bureaus

Hypothesis 3 has several sub-hypotheses that address different aspects of this question. The first states that the existence of a credit bureau should increase the poverty reduction effect of microfinance. The argument here is based on the availability of information. The more an MFI knows about a potential customer, the better able they are to efficiently allocate loans and to avoid risky borrowers. This is critical for the institution's finances. Even the most socially oriented MFI must carefully manage its finances or face the prospects of losing too much money and being forced to close. So even when financial performance is not the primary objective, it will always be a significant concern for MFI managers because many MFIs operate on very thin margins, and must struggle to secure enough capital to continue expanding operations and offering more financial services to more people (Schicks 2007). Having more information about borrowers allows MFIs to offer loans to more reliable customers who are more likely to repay their loans. When they do not have resources tied up in delinquent loans, the MFI can offer more loans to more perspective borrowers.

Credit bureaus are also a benefit to the customers because the MFIs are able to help avoid over-indebtedness (Khan 2009). Some customers might know how much they can afford to borrow, but many may not know what a safe debt-to-income ratio might be. Having a functioning credit bureau would help the MFI better serve the customers' needs by helping them manage their debt. Also, having a functioning credit bureau would allow MFI customers to court different financial service providers (Karlan and Goldberg 2011). A customer might start with one MFI that offers small loans, then move on to another institution that offers larger loans once the customer has proven herself a reliable borrower. Some scholars argue that graduating borrowers to larger loans with more profitable terms as income grows should be an objective of all MFIs (Ahlin, Jiang, and Paper 2005). Microfinance is meant to help the poor by alleviating some of the pain of poverty and, eventually, to help remove them from poverty. If this is to happen, at some point they will need financial services from other institutions, but in order to be considered for traditional financial services, they will need some way of proving that they are reliable borrowers.

Credit bureaus come in two basic genres. They can be either public or private. Publicly operated credit bureaus are more likely to focus their data collection efforts on commercial banks or other significant financial institutions. Private credit registries are more likely to collect data from the retail industry, non-banking lenders, credit card companies, credit cooperatives and other similar institutions (Miller 2000). The two variables *Public* and *Private* each report the percentage of adults who are covered by public or private credit registries.

Using regression analysis, we can look at the data to see how credit bureau coverage affects microfinance impact. Put another way, we are interested in whether credit bureau coverage changes the effect of microfinance on poverty. So, it may be that where credit bureau coverage is broad, microfinance has a big impact on poverty, but where credit bureau coverage is minimal, the problems associated with lack of information may impede the poverty alleviation impact we would otherwise expect from microfinance. Capturing this dynamic requires the use of an interaction term in the regression to capture how varying levels of credit bureau coverage interact with varying levels of microfinance and what their joint impact on poverty is. In the regression this is accomplished by simply multiplying the two terms together.

Another obstacle to regression analysis is endogeneity. Microfinance affects poverty, but poverty also affects microfinance. That is, microfinance helps the poor by providing them capital and giving them an opportunity to raise their income level. However, it might also be the case that MFIs are more attracted to countries with more poverty. If this is the case, it will introduce bias into the regression and make the results unreliable. The commonly accepted correction is to use instrumental variables to stand in place of the endogenous explanatory variable. The previous year's total microfinance assets and average outreach are used to instrument for the number of borrowers. These make useful instrumental variables because the microfinance industry's pool of assets imposes a limit on how many loans the industry can make. The size of the asset pool is not driven by poverty, but by the size and strength of the financial sector, regulation and foreign funding of microfinance (*see chapter 6*). Using lagged assets adds another degree of separation between poverty and the number of borrowers because this year's poverty level cannot affect last year's pool of assets.

Outreach is an indicator of the degree to which MFIs service the financial needs of the rural and minority populations. Setting up a branch in an urban slum will open financial services for a lot of people, but it may also be duplicating services offered by other MFIs, and adding little benefit to the community. Therefore, an MFI that was able to extend service to a disempowered group who might not otherwise have access to financial services because they are oppressed in some way would score better on outreach measures. Alternatively, an MFI that extended services to a previously unserved rural population would also score high on outreach. So, greater outreach means that the microfinance industry is offering financial services to more people. The combination of outreach and lagged assets will be used as instrumental variables for the number of borrowers for all subsequent regressions. Tables will report only the second stage results.

Regression analysis suggests that credit registry coverage does not change the impact of microfinance. Greater credit registry coverage appears to have a positive impact on poverty, even after controlling for a host of other variables, but it does not interact with microfinance. So, having a more comprehensive credit registry must influence poverty through some channel other than microfinance. If we assume that simply having more adults covered by a credit registry does not spontaneously reduce poverty, we are led to think about how credit bureaus reduce poverty. One answer may be that the types of entities that are likely to consult credit registries and are also likely to interact with the poor are consumer credit providers, be they merchants or traditional financial institutions (Miller 2000). The poor can access credit without going to MFIs.

This result casts some real doubt on the microfinance effect. Examining table 4.3 shows that the microfinance measure did not, independently, have a statistically significant impact on poverty in either regression. We can deduct from the impact of credit bureau coverage that the poor are influenced by finance, but not by the microfinance industry. This means that the poor need financial services, access financial services, and benefit from access to those financial services, but microfinance is not part of the equation. They are going elsewhere to meet their financial needs. Microfinance is not filling the niche that it was created to fill. It is not providing financial services to the poor in a way that helps the poor make their way out of poverty. Something other than microfinance is doing what microfinance proponents claim microfinance is accomplishing.

Thus, we begin to question the entire microfinance model. If the needs of the poor are being met from somewhere other than the microfinance industry, then what is the microfinance industry doing? If they are servicing the poor, their services are, according to the data, not helpful for alleviating poverty. Perhaps this is because interest rates are so high that any benefits the poor might gain from microfinancial services are sucked up in interest payments, or maybe it is because most microfinance customers use their loans not for

Table 4.3. **Credit Registry and Law-Order**

| | Change in Infant Mortality | | |
|---|---|---|---|
| | *(1)* | *(2)* | *(3)* |
| Number of borrowers | 0.00224 | 0.000737 | 0.0135** |
| | (0.00249) | (0.00193) | (0.00520) |
| Private credit bureau | −0.00174*** | | |
| | (0.000493) | | |
| Number * Private credit | −0.0000511 | | |
| | (0.0000376) | | |
| Public credit bureau | | −0.00934** | |
| | | (0.00316) | |
| Number * Public credit | | 0.0000278 | |
| | | (0.000168) | |
| Law and Order | | | 0.0892*** |
| | | | (0.0242) |
| Number * Law and Order | | | −0.00463* |
| | | | (0.00192) |
| FDI | 0.631 | 0.393 | −0.996 |
| | (0.890) | (0.823) | (0.579) |
| Foreign Aid | −0.256 | −0.123 | 0.764** |
| | (0.786) | (0.405) | (0.247) |
| Static infant mortality | −0.0424*** | −0.0429*** | −0.0413*** |
| | (0.00233) | (0.00283) | (0.00156) |
| Polity2 democracy score | −0.0160 | −0.0170** | 0.0214 |
| | (0.0103) | (0.00568) | (0.0157) |
| Constant | 0.220 | 0.258* | −0.415*** |
| | (0.121) | (0.115) | (0.122) |
| $R^2$ | 0.531 | 0.544 | 0.647 |
| chi2 | 920.9 | 964.3 | 2070.6 |
| N | 125 | 128 | 302 |

Standard errors in parentheses, * $p < 0.05$, ** $p < 0.01$, *** $p < 0.001$
Panel Corrected Standard Errors using 2nd Stage Instrumental Variable Regression (Number = l.assets * out_reach)

so-called *productive* purposes but for consumer purchases (Bateman 2013; Roodman 2012). On the other hand, the problem might lie in who is actually using microfinance. It may be that the very poor do not have the business experience, connections or resources to make effective use of microfinance so the not-so-poor, those above the poverty line, are using microfinance as a convenient credit option (Annim 2012).

## Hypothesis 2 Again

This first group of models also serves as the first test of hypothesis 2, that microfinance will reduce poverty under any conditions. This was an easy hurdle for microfinance that it failed to clear. The models controlled for some of the other major explanations of, and programs for, poverty alleviation in order to distinguish between the effects of microfinance and the other explanations. If anything, this represents only a minimal set of control variables to account for alternative explanations.

Of course, credit bureau coverage was also included in the model, but credit bureau coverage was not even expected to have a direct impact on microfinance. Rather, it was expected to enhance the impact of microfinance. It is not a competing explanation, but a complementary explanation, which made this a low hurdle. A country with good credit registry coverage that would allow microfinance customers to transition smoothly to traditional commercial services should have presented optimal conditions for microfinance. Either the logic surrounding credit registry coverage is faulty, the analysis is fatally flawed, or microfinance is a rather ineffective poverty alleviation approach.

Credit bureaus differ from *Law and Order* and *Stability* in that credit bureaus are designed to make exclusion easier. They serve the interests of profitability, which often conflicts with serving the interests of the poor. On the other hand, *Law and Order* and *Stability* are both public goods and, for the most part, non-excludable. Therefore, it is not unreasonable to think that the results from these two areas will offer more useful conclusions than for credit registry coverage.

## Strong Law and Order

The next sub-hypothesis is that a stronger Law and Order should make microfinance a more efficient poverty alleviation mechanism. There are two elements to the concept of *Law and Order*. The first is a well-functioning court system. That is, a court system that is unbiased, relatively independent of politics and procedurally sound. An independent court system is crucial for entrepreneurialism and investment. Independent courts protect property rights through contract enforcement and efficient institutions which regulate private capture and limit corruption by ensuring equal treatment and discouraging rent-seeking behavior (Haggard and Tiede 2011). This is the institution that protects citizens from the state and the weak from the powerful. Since the poor are, individually, politically weak, a well-functioning court system should serve to protect their interests. An independent court serves as an unbiased platform for judging grievances or disputes based on the merits of the case rather than wealth or political influence, which is unlikely to occur in the absence of a well-functioning court system.

The second element is an effective law enforcement body; police who patrol the streets to deter crime, investigate crime and apprehend criminals.

Law and order mitigates violence and affords a degree of personal security and protection of personal property. Douglas North, winner of the 1993 Nobel Prize in Economics, wrote that "the inability of societies to develop effective, low-cost enforcement of contracts is the most important source of both historical stagnation and contemporary underdevelopment in the third World" (North 1990; Trebilcock and Leng 2010). It is the rule of law that removes a society from Hobbes' state of nature. Research suggests that strong law and order may be "the most efficient solution to the problem of insecurity of property and contracting in a modern economy" (Haggard, MacIntyre, and Tiede 2008).

Corruption and rent seeking are not only unproductive, they are counter-productive, since the cumbersomeness of the system cuts away at production efficiency when business owners are forced to slog through messy government bureaucracy and pay arbitrary fees in order to make things happen (Acemoglu and Robinson 2012). A strong law and order, which ensures private property rights, incentivizes innovation and investment. Citizens and entrepreneurs can be more confident that they will not be subject to arbitrary seizures and that they will be able to keep a larger portion of any efficiency gains they can create through their innovativeness. The logical extreme is a situation where people have no confidence that they will be able to retain control of their profits or property, as happened with many of the former European colonies. Indigenous peoples were often enslaved, in one fashion or another, and stripped of any surplus they could produce (Baker 2014). Consequently, they produced only what they needed to survive in the short-term and nothing more. This example shows what can be avoided, or at least reduced, with strong law and order. It will also reduce at least a portion of the predatory behavior that is commonly found in developing countries, and thereby lessen the proportion of potentially productive labor devoted to guarding against theft and other drains on society. For the microfinance customer, this means that she can be more confident that her property will remain in her possession and undamaged and that government bureaucracy will not impose undue burdens.

The empirical analysis supports the expected impact of microfinance. The results in table 4.3 show that, independent of law and order, microfinance does not reduce poverty. It also shows that law and order alone does not reduce poverty. However, the interaction of law and order with microfinance has a statistically significant effect on poverty. Unfortunately, one of the difficulties with regressing interaction terms is interpreting the results. The beta coefficient gives two-dimensional information about a three-dimensional relationship. In order to get a clearer picture of how law and order interacts with microfinance, look at figure 4.1. The three different lines show the predicted

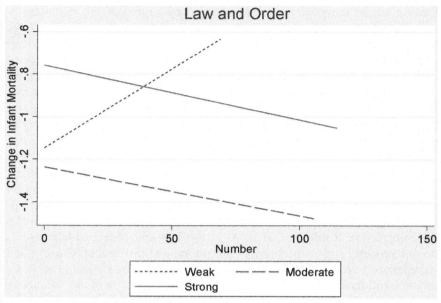

Figure 4.1.    The Effects of Law and Order

linear relationship between the number of borrowers and infant mortality at different levels of law and order.[2]

From the figure we can conclude that not only does law and order interact significantly with microfinance, it approximates the expected relationship. Where law and order is strong, or at least moderate, higher levels of microfinance seem to reduce infant mortality. Where law and order is weak, however, not only does microfinance not reduce infant mortality, it may actually increase it. This may be because it is under these conditions where potential microfinance clients are most vulnerable and, perhaps, most desperate. Their vulnerability leaves them fully exposed to the risks of entrepreneurship (Chang 2012). They likely receive little or no government help to retain personal property, or to get their microenterprise off the ground or personal financial protection if it fails. On the other hand, because conditions are so poor, these same people are desperate to improve their situation. Their desperation may lead them to take on imprudent risks; perhaps risking too much, or investing in an excessively risky venture. The end result is that people living in countries where the law and order is the weakest are not only the least likely to be productive with their loans, they are mostly likely to suffer if they run into financial hardships.

In countries where the law and order is the weakest, increasing the number of microfinance borrowers from zero to fifty borrowers per thousand population is predicted to raise the rate of infant mortality by almost four per 10,000 live births, all else being equal. But, where law and order is modest or better, the same increase in microfinance borrowers is expected to decrease the infant mortality rate by about one per 10,000 live births. This is an enormous increase in microfinance, akin from going from no microfinance at all to having an industry like that of Colombia or Ecuador around 2009. Fifty borrowers per thousand population represents about the 90th percentile of the most comprehensive microfinance industries. This kind of shift takes years to build. Colombia's microfinance industry had only reached about 0.5 borrowers per thousand population in 1996 when it began to grow quite rapidly. It took thirteen years to reach the fifty borrowers per thousand population mark. Many countries have never achieved this level of microfinance. Costa Rica's industry first recorded borrowers in 1998, but by 2010 there were still only about five borrowers per thousand population.

So microfinance can reduce poverty, at least under some conditions, though certainly not all conditions. Using microfinance as a poverty alleviation mechanism is expensive though. It requires tremendous assets to increase the number of borrowers by the margins specified above. In most countries with around fifty borrowers per thousand population, the microfinance industry has the equivalent of about five percent of GDP in microfinance assets. For Ecuador in 2010, a country of just fifteen million people and GDP per capita just over US$1,700, 5% of GDP is the equivalent of about US$ 1.25 billion. That is more than twenty-five times as much FDI or foreign aid as the country received in the same year. It is certainly possible to increase microfinance assets to those levels, but it requires time and a lot of resources. The return, however, is quite marginal.

So, the data supports sub-hypothesis B and the idea that the effectiveness of microfinance as a poverty alleviation mechanism depends on the conditions in which it is operating, though the effect of microfinance under poor conditions can be very damaging and under the best conditions only slightly useful. Next, we move on to look at whether political and economic stability affect microfinance in the same ways as law and order.

## Systemic Stability

Another important characteristic of a country, which might affect the microfinance industry, is the degree of stability in government policies and institutions. Political and economic stability are intimately related since the government plays a major role in promoting economic stability and economic stability often plays a major role in promoting satisfaction with the government and, therefore, its longevity. Political stability accounts for extreme conditions such as war, but also more common conditions including ethnic and religious tensions, the role of the military in politics, and the stability of the regime.[3] Internal tensions can lead to protests or riots that may have a significant impact on a household's ability to earn an income. Latin American history shows how destabilizing it can be to have the military meddling in politics. It erodes the democratic process and can significantly change policies and institutions.

Economic stability includes a host of variables from the stability of the currency to the stability of interest rates, exchange rates, tax rates and so on.[4] It also includes the degree of variation in economic growth rates. The more interest rates or inflation go up and down, the less confident a microentrepreneur or a household can be that it is either getting a better rate now than it could if it waited a few months, or that an investment now will be an asset rather than a liability in a few months. The more certain an actor can be of future profits, the more efficiently she can maximize her investment portfolio today. Governments play a major role in promoting, even creating, economic stability, and economic stability plays a major role in individual- or household-level financial decisions. Potential microfinance customers or entrepreneurs should be more hesitant to start a microenterprise if they are uncertain whether they will be able to turn a profit and repay their loan on time if the business climate should sour (Islam 2009).

The interaction between microfinance and political instability shown in table 4.4 is statistically significant at the 90% confidence level. The visual representation of the interaction effect in figure 4.2 shows that the relationship is just as expected based on the discussion from chapter 3.[5] Indeed, as with *Law and Order*, at the highest level of risk for political instability, higher levels of microfinance are predicted to put a slight upward pressure on infant mortality. Where risk for instability is modest, a marginal increase in microfinance is expected to slightly reduce infant mortality rates, but the same increase in the most stable states dramatically reduces infant mortality rates. Again, this means that people in the least stable states are more likely to see a decrease in their standard of living, rather than an increase, when they participate in microfinance. The reverse is true for even moderate levels of *Political Stability*, although these people are still not likely to see significant improvements in their standard of living either, all else being equal.

To put this into numbers, among the least stable countries, increasing the number of microfinance borrowers has a negligible effect on infant mortality. In moderately stable states increasing the number of borrowers from zero to 50 per thousand population is predicted to decrease infant mortality by about .5 per 10,000 live births. Only those microfinance clients who live in the most stable states are likely to see their standard of living improve significantly

**Table 4.4.　Political and Economic Stability**

| | Change in Infant Mortality | |
|---|---|---|
| | *(1)* | *(2)* |
| Number of borrowers | 0.00906** | 0.00838** |
| | (0.00307) | (0.00280) |
| Political Stability | −0.00404 | |
| | (0.00255) | |
| Number * Political Stability | −0.000117** | |
| | (0.0000422) | |
| Economic Stability | | −0.00592 |
| | | (0.00437) |
| Number * Economic Stability | | −0.000174** |
| | | (0.0000672) |
| FDI | −0.994 | −1.083* |
| | (0.544) | (0.509) |
| Foreign aid | 1.157*** | 0.783** |
| | (0.269) | (0.260) |
| Polity2 democracy score | 0.0409** | 0.0318* |
| | (0.0150) | (0.0133) |
| Static infant mortality | −0.0435*** | −0.0429*** |
| | (0.00138) | (0.00128) |
| constant | 0.0158 | 0.0117 |
| | (0.155) | (0.159) |
| $R^2$ | 0.662 | 0.658 |
| chi2 | 4537.4 | 3883.2 |
| N | 302 | 302 |

Standard errors in parentheses, * $p < 0.05$, ** $p < 0.01$, *** $p < 0.001$
Panel Corrected Standard Errors using 2nd Stage Instrumental Variable Regression (Number = l.assets * out_reach)

through microfinance. In these countries the same increase in the number of microfinance borrowers is expected to reduce infant mortality by about 2.5 per 10,000 live births.

The effects of economic stability are even more pronounced. The general pattern is the same, where instability turns microfinance negative and stability makes it a positive influence on poverty. Using the same increase in the number of borrowers as above in the least stable states is predicted to increase infant mortality by about 2.5 per 10,000 live births. However, the same treatment in moderately stable states decreases infant mortality by about two deaths and in the most stable states it decreases by 3.5 deaths per 10,000 live births. Economic stability has the greatest potential for reducing infant mortality, but its effect is smaller than the harm done by weak law and order, which has the potential to increase infant mortality by approximately 4, under the same parameters.

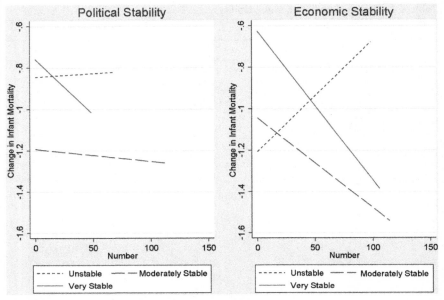

**Figure 4.2.   The Effects of Political and Economic Stability**

## WHAT THIS MEANS IN THE REAL WORLD

Based on these results, there are a number of countries in Latin America that should be leery of microfinance, and other that may benefit from it. For example, Brazil suffers from weak law and order. Although Brazil's economy is usually in the very stable category and political stability is at least moderate, the negative effects of weak law and order overwhelm the benefits of microfinance we could expect from political and economic stability. The model predicts that in the best years, microfinance in Brazil would contribute weakly to poverty alleviation and in the worst years it could significantly exacerbate poverty in the country.

On the other hand, the model predicts that Bolivia should see much benefit from microfinance. It has one of the most saturated microfinance markets in Latin America. Bolivia's economy is generally very stable, though its political system is only moderately stable and law and order is only moderate. Research suggests, and the data support, that microfinance has some impact on poverty, marginally raising incomes for most borrowers (Mosley 2001).[6] Peru is the only other country that compares with Bolivia in terms of market saturation, but it is in the same boat, with a very stable economy, but only a moderately stable political system and moderate law and order. Peru and Bolivia may be seeing infant mortality rates as much as ten fewer infant deaths per 10,000 live births due to the poverty alleviating effect of microfinance in each country. This represents a roughly 2.5% decrease for Bolivia, which has a relatively high infant mortality rate of approximately four hundred per 10,000 live births. Peru has one of the lowest infant mortality rates in the region, though, at less than 150. So the same nominal decrease in Peru represents a much larger, though still modest, 6.6% decline in infant mortality. These changes are modest when we consider the value of assets that are tied up in the programs. Microfinance assets totaled nearly US$ 4 billion in Bolivia for 2011, and more than US$ 10 billion for Peru.

Of course, some of the money that funds the microfinance industry came from government agencies, but much of it came from the private sector. Total government funding for the microfinance industry in Bolivia in 2011 was about US$ 26 million, only a fraction of the total US$ 600 million of funding from all sources. In Peru the story is nearly identical, with government funding making up about 4% of the total US$ 1.9 billion in funding, at US$ 80 million.

These two Andes-region countries differ from many of their neighbors though. Paraguay, for example, has tried following Bolivia and Peru in regards to microfinance, but conditions there are far less conducive to microfinance having the desired impact. Paraguay's economy and political system are only moderately stable, but law and order is weak. Consequently, the cumulative effect is to harm the poor, rather than help them. Nonetheless, Paraguay's microfinance industry received US$ 180 million total in funding in 2011, but government funding accounted for four times as much at US$ 24 million. Government agencies are funding organizations that are likely counter-productive.

## CONCLUSION

This chapter began by explaining how the hypotheses from chapter 3 would be tested. The hypotheses have been tested against the data and the results are mixed. The data partially supported hypothesis 1, which stated that better government institutions would help reduce poverty. The analysis showed that government institutions related directly to the economy mattered while other institutions, such as public health spending and infrastructure, did not have a statistically significant impact on infant mortality. The conclusion is that solid economic performance matters more for poverty alleviation than do less directly related institutions. If people have more money, they can pay for better healthcare and do not have to rely on public health spending. People benefit more from a well-performing economy than from greater access to education, at least in the short term. Economic institutions have the greatest short-term impact on poverty.

It was not necessary to carry out an independent test of hypothesis 2 because if it was true that microfinance helped alleviate poverty under all conditions, then it should have manifested such through the tests of hypothesis 3. Hypothesis 2 was flatly rejected. There were some conditions under which microfinance seemed to help alleviate poverty, but there were several tests where the data showed that some conditions prevented microfinance from alleviating poverty, and even exacerbated it. This is, in some respects, a relief for the field of microfinance because, although it would be earth-moving to find the silver bullet for poverty, the evidence on microfinance so far has been mixed, despite the rhetoric coming from many advocates. Now there is empirical evidence showing one reason that the evidence may be mixed and how microfinance can be made more effective. What many experts have failed to acknowledge previously is that the impact of microfinance depends on the conditions in which it is operating. The results found here have led to this conclusion. Almost nothing in social science always works, under all conditions. Nor does something gain as much approbation as microfinance has without producing results for at least some segment of the population. Microfinance is no different.

Finally, hypothesis 3 tested some of the specific government institutions that were expected to influence the impact of microfinance. Again, the results were mixed. Credit registries had no impact on microfinance. Perhaps the connection between microfinance and traditional finance is too tenuous, so microfinance customers do not graduate to traditional finance and, therefore, are not greatly impacted by institutions that are designed for the commercial finance sector. Law and order does have a significant impact on microfinance though. A country with strong law and order can expect to benefit from microfinance. However, in a country with weak law and order, the effect of microfinance, in relation to the poor, reverses, making them worse off through microfinance. In fact, the negative impact of microfinance under weak law and order is considerably larger than the positive impact in a country with strong law and order.

Unfortunately, poor people in countries with weak law and order want to improve their financial situation just as badly as their peers in strong law and order countries. Therefore, they may be just as likely to take loans from MFIs. A state that suffers from weak law and order also likely suffers from weak state capacity to create and enforce regulations on the microfinance industry that might protect the poor, or to offer alternatives to microfinance. A state can improve law and order, of course, but it is generally a long and difficult process that typically takes several years to accomplish. It is not a quick fix a state can implement to make the microfinance industry immediately more effective. On the other hand, strong law and order will, of course, impact far more than just microfinance and will reduce poverty in other ways as well.

Political and economic stability both have a statistically significant impact on microfinance effectiveness. As expected, greater stability engenders a stronger poverty alleviation effect through microfinance. Where hypothesis 1 showed that economic performance contributed to poverty alleviation, independent of microfinance, hypothesis three illustrates that it also helps make microfinance a more effective tool for poverty alleviation. However, like law and order, economic instability turns the microfinance impact negative. Poor people in economically unstable countries are more likely to be made worse off through microfinance than better off. Though, once again, improving economic and political stability is not easy or quick.

Perhaps one of the most important conclusions we can draw from this chapter is that microfinance works, but only sometimes. It is not likely to benefit the poorest of the poor, the poor in unstable or poorly governed countries, but rather people in more stable, better-governed countries. Somewhat ironically, the very poor are precisely the people who most need help with poverty alleviation, who should benefit most from capital influx, according to neoliberal economic theory. Bad governance prevents them from capturing the potential gains microfinance might otherwise offer. Instead, microfinance is more likely to benefit people in more stable, better-governed countries where there are likely other programs and other alternatives to microfinance; countries where the government is relatively effective at improving and maintaining optimal conditions for economic growth and poverty alleviation.

Hopefully, this chapter has provided some useful insights, drawn from the empirical analysis. The benefit of the large N analysis is that we can look at broad patterns that occur or persist across time and across borders. This satellite view provides useful information for studying the effectiveness of microfinance. However, sometimes key details are lost with such a broad view. Therefore, the next chapter looks at the microfinance industry in a single country. Narrowing the focus to a single case allows for a more detail-rich analysis of how government institutions might change how microfinance impacts the poor.

## NOTES

1. Universal primary education was one of the millennium development goals. Primary education rates have been increasing for quite some time, and now, in 2015, the

world is very close to achieving this goal in most regions, including Latin America. However, there was still a reasonable amount of variation across Latin America up to at least 2010.

2. Law and order is measured on a scale from 0 to 6 in intervals of .5, and with a mean just under 3. Weak law and order is anything less than 3, which is the modal category. Anything above 3 was classified as strong law and order.

3. The International Country Risk Guide measure of Political Stability used here includes government stability, or the goverment's ability to implement policies and to stay in office; socioeconomic conditions, which might fuel social dissatisfaction; the investment profile; internal and external conflict; corruption; military in politics; religious tensions; law and order; ethnic tensions; democratic accountability; and bureaucracy quality.

4. The International Country Risk Guide measure of Economic Stability used here includes GDP/capita; real GDP growth; the annual inflation rate; budget balance as a percentage of GDP; and the current account balance as a percentage of GDP.

5. For political stability, anything below 55, or approximately the bottom quartile, was classified as unstable, 55–68 is moderately stable, and above 68, which is the upper quartile, is very stable. For economic stability, the cut points are 30 and 37, which, again, approximately represent the upper and lower quartiles. Results do not change significantly with minor variations in the cut points used.

6. Mosley notes that crises, even small crises, can be catastrophic for many borrowers because they tend to be highly leveraged. This makes borrowers highly vulnerable. Those who experience even modest financial problems can be thrown back into poverty because their debt service ratios are so high (Mosley 2001).

# Chapter Five

# Microfinance in Brazil

## A Case Study

This chapter will examine the relationships between microfinance and government institutions at a different level. Where chapter 4 approached the topic from a large N statistical perspective, studying all of Latin America over approximately 10 years, this chapter focuses on a single case: Brazil. Brazil was selected because it is, in many ways, representative of much of Latin America. As a country, it is in the middle of the pack of Latin American countries for microfinance saturation. Its political climate has undergone changes over the past few decades not unlike the changes that several other countries in the region have experienced, and economic and financial risk factors have varied along with the political changes. This provides useful data for scrutiny and analysis. Brazil is an interesting case to study because its risk factors vary widely over time as well as geography. Brazil's industrial and economic development has been a tumultuous process. In the most recent phase of this process, during most of the 1990s and the first few years of the 2000s, Brazil was given relatively high risk scores across the board. During the middle of that decade scores improved significantly, only to drop again before recovering towards the end of the decade.

Also, as a federal state there are sub-units within Brazil that can be studied independently, thus allowing for a deeper analysis. Geographically, Brazil developed very unevenly. Consequently it is often broken into five regions; the North and Northeast are the poorest regions. The North is poor because it is in the heart of the Amazon basin where rivers and thick forest make travel difficult. The Northeast was home to most of Brazil's sugar plantations in the eighteenth and early nineteenth centuries and today has the highest density of poverty and low industrial output. The Central West is the country's breadbasket. The Southeast and South have been the industrial and financial center of the country for generations, with relatively robust economies and low poverty rates. This makes for useful comparisons between the different regions of Brazil.

Where chapter 4 studied all three hypotheses derived from the theory in chapter 3, this chapter will focus on the third hypothesis, which deals with the three risk factors and their effects on poverty reduction through microfinance. The government institutions hypothesis is the focus here because this is where this research contributes the most to the field. As in the previous chapter, I assume that instability and risk for future instability are good indicators of the quality of governmental institutions since good institutions should be able to minimize risk.

Hypothesis 3: The higher the quality of governmental institutions, the greater the poverty reduction effect of microfinance.

## A BRIEF HISTORY OF RECENT POLITICAL CHANGES IN BRAZIL

Although Brazilian history extends back to the sixteenth century, from the time that the aristocracy lost control of the leadership in Brazil, the country experienced cycles of tremendous economic growth and periods of severe mismanagement. Getúlio Vargas became the country's provisional president in 1930. Before that time Brazil had been primarily an agricultural economy, exporting tropical and sub-tropical products primarily to the North Atlantic states (Skidmore 1967). Some of these products are rubber, coffee, tobacco, cocoa, cotton and tropical fruits. Coffee was a uniquely important cash crop that the federal government depended on for tax revenue. The trouble was that the world market price of coffee began to decline considerably around Vargas' time. Vargas continued the policies of his predecessors, trying to manipulate the world coffee market in order to maintain higher prices for coffee. The government regularly purchased large quantities of coffee from growers, which it withheld from the market, assuming that global demand was relatively inelastic (Baer 2001). Where this strategy had only been moderately successful before 1930, it seems to have been more successful during the depression years. The result was a current account surplus for Brazil during the mid- to late 1930s.

Although Vargas was a proud *Gaucho* from the southern state of Rio Grande do Sul, as interim president, and then dictator after 1937, he was concerned with making all of Brazil more productive and stable (Skidmore 1967). He was the first president to travel to many of the rural regions of the North and Central West plains, and the first to show any real interest in the Northeast since the demand for Brazilian sugar had all but died nearly a century before. Vargas encouraged increased agricultural productivity, but he also advocated for industrialization. He may have been one of the first Latin American leaders to follow Import Substitution Industrialization (ISI) policies. With the current account surplus largely from coffee receipts from the mid-1930s Brazil began to buy industrial technology and equipment hoping to boost industrial manufacturing (Baer 2001). Vargas also courted FDI, which helped industrialize the country as investors brought in new technology, equipment and best practices (Amann 2003; Levine 1998). Celso Furtado, one of Brazil's most recognized and distinguished economists, said that this period, beginning in 1930, is when the industrial system was implanted in Brazil (Dulles 2014).

Another of Vargas' legacies was his attention to the plight of the poor. He created a meritocratic hiring process for the civil service in which anybody and everybody could take civil service exams (Levine 1998). Hiring was based on qualifications, regardless of race. Vargas did not go out of his way to hire people of color, but neither did he discriminate against them, which they saw as a welcome change. This meant that an entire cohort of the population had opportunities opened to them that had never been available before. Vargas also instituted a minimum wage and mandatory benefits for salaried workers (Dulles 2014; Skidmore 1967). He organized *Sindicatos*, or officially recognized unions to represent workers (Levine 1998; Skidmore 1967). He did all of this to try and close the wealth and income gaps in Brazil, and to grow the Brazilian economy.

Vargas' close relationship with US president Franklin D. Roosevelt during the war years meant that Brazil cooperated fairly extensively with the United States. Roosevelt sent US Army maintenance personnel to improve airports and construct buildings and roads all over Brazil (Levine 1998). Brazil increased production of iron ore, rubber and other raw materials for the Allied war effort. Steel mills and chemical plants were built and rail lines and other infrastructure were improved so Brazil could begin producing steel, petrochemicals and fertilizer for the Allies as well (Novelli and Galvão 2001). Brazil grew its industrial sector with export profits and through state investments. This represents the first period of ISI.

However, because of the massive US spending in Brazil, and her exports to other Allied states, Brazil got its first taste of inflation, which would become a recurring problem in the Brazilian economy for the following 50 years (Baer 2001). Vargas adjusted the minimum wage to account for inflation and authorized the legislature to punish speculators in foodstuffs in order to keep prices on essential goods in check (Dulles 2014). These policies were moderately effective, preventing inflation from leaving the poor in complete destitution, but were unable to reduce inflation to levels that would be conducive to real growth. By the end of the war Brazil had several state-of-the-art steel mills, paper mills, and petrochemical plants, and had discovered oil. Nonetheless, the authoritarian Vargas was pushed out of office and a new democratic regime was created.

The first post-war election brought in General Dutra. Politically, Dutra was rather bland. Economically he began by opening the economy, removing trade barriers and liberalizing exchange rates. The result was that by 1947 Brazil had virtually exhausted its foreign exchange reserves and gone from huge current account surpluses to major current account deficits (Skidmore 1967). He subsequently reintroduced exchange controls and spent the rest of his term in office addressing short-term issues. Regardless of his apparently stumbling policies, Brazil continued to industrialize through the late 1940s until Vargas returned to the capital in Rio de Janeiro as the democratically elected president in 1950.

Vargas and his successors continued many of the same economic policies as before, courting FDI to promote industrialization. ISI continued, often helped along by foreign exchange controls, which shifted over time in response to waves of inflation, exhausted foreign reserves, and government budgetary deficits (Skidmore, Smith, and Green 2014). Although industrialization moved forward, urbanization, inflation and growing inequality together countered many of the benefits of industrialization for the working poor (Baer 2001). Prices on basic consumer goods, like food and housing, outstripped wage growth so that real wages declined. The national poverty rate in 1970 reached 68%, one of the highest ever recorded by Brazil's Instituto de Pesquisa e Economia Aplicada (IPEA).

In 1964 the military took control of the state once again, riding a wave of support in large part due to the economic pressure many Brazilians were facing and their dissatisfaction with the democratic regime. The military regime quickly moved to try and improve the economy since it was the risk of working-class militancy that gave legitimacy to the 1964 coup (Meade 2010). However, the military regime did not change course. Rather than reversing the ISI policies implemented by civilian leaders, the military doubled down on ISI. As often happens when an economy experiences a massive stimulus, the economy grew dramatically for a few years, before falling into a slump.

General Emilio Medici launched what has often been called the "Brazilian Miracle." The regime made a renewed effort to court foreign investment in order to boost manufacturing and to build infrastructure. Brazil also opened its borders to trade in a way it never had before (Baer 2001). The result was that GDP more than tripled from 1965 to 1980 (Frieden 1987). Steel production and automobile manufacturing increased by factors of 3 and 5, respectively (Meade 2010). The true "Miracle Years" were 1968–1973, during which the economy saw double-digit growth and inflation held below 20% (Alves 1985). Most of the miracle was in the industrial sector, but tax deductions for capital gains also spurred the stock market as well. Foreign investments grew from $11.4 million in 1968 to $4.5 billion by 1973.

The problem was that these gains were due, almost exclusively, to foreign debt, with very little domestic investment. Initially the economy was able to export enough to service debt obligations, but as debt continued to increase, and more and more Brazilians moved to the cities to look for work, combined with the oil crises of the 1970s, the system's weak foundation quickly began to fracture. Between 1980 and 1983 GDP per capita fell by 15% and the capital goods industry finished out 1983 at 60% of what it had been just three years earlier (Frieden 1987). Needless to say, many Brazilians suffered when the "Brazilian Miracle" turned into the Brazilian nightmare. This was also a period of tremendous inequality, with the wealthy capturing most of the profits from growth and the poor uninsulated against the downward slide of the economy (Vanden and Prevost 2015). Inequality persisted despite the ups and downs of the economy, but the economic lows were particularly painful for the poor because they generally had little or no savings, and nothing with which to ameliorate the effects of economic decline (Amann 2003).

Reported poverty rates improved considerably from 1970 to 1980, although it was still rather high in 1980 at nearly 40%. Some of the improvement was the result of the miracle growth years, but some of it was also the result of under-reporting poverty (Alves 1985). In 1975 an estimated 25 million children were living without their most basic needs being met, and 68% of children in one study reported working more than forty hours per week to supplement the family's income (Alves 1985). Hunger became a serious concern for many Brazilians. The World Bank commissioned a report on hunger and undernourishment in Brazil. It concluded that malnourishment was the cause of 40% of infant mortality, which was at an astonishingly high 87.3/1,000 live births. The same report found that 79.5% of Northeasterners consumed less than the UN established minimum caloric intake for human development, as did 87.4% of people in Northern states, and even 57.9% in Southeastern and Southern states. Despite an increase in minimum salaries in 1983, a minimum salary was not enough to pay for the basic caloric needs of an adult man, much less housing, clothes, transportation, or the needs of an entire family. Much of the pain the poor were facing during this time was the result of inflation and government over-indebtedness (Baer 2001; Bresser-Pereira 2002).

General Ernesto Geisel won the presidency in 1974 with the announced policy of returning to democratic rule (Chaffee 2015). The military government loosened restriction on political parties, hoping that the growing opposition would fracture into multiple parties that would be incapable of challenging the incumbent military regime (Weeks 2015). Instead it led to *abertura* or "opening" of the political system. Elections were held within a few years and civilian control returned. However, a series of unfortunate events prevented potentially successful leaders from making meaningful changes for nearly another decade. President-elect Tancredo Neves, who many people thought was capable of turning the economy around, died in April 1985 before he was able to enter office. Consequently, his vice president, José Sarney, who was not nearly as popular or prepared to fill the role, was made president (Amann 2003; Roett 2011). Brazil suffered from rampant inflation, a stagnating economy, and lingering human rights abuses being perpetrated by government actors, even after the democratic transition (Meade 2010). Government debt approached 55% of GDP in 1988, one of the highest debt-to-GDP ratios in the world at that time (Martone 2003). The inflation that was already marring the economy worsened over time. The military government grew the economy via a massive influx of borrowed capital, but when debt obligations began to outstrip the government's ability to raise revenue the economy went into a tailspin of ever increasing inflation as the state printed cash to try and cover its debt. In the 1970s inflation was around 74%, which grew to 428% in the 1980s, and reached 1400% from 1990 to 1994 (Gordon 2001, 3). Inflation, of course, eroded real wages, which quickly drove the prices of key commodities, especially food, out of reach for many Brazilian households (Bresser-Pereira 2009). Change in the price index topped out at 1061.5% in 1988 (Amann 2003).

In response to the economic problems that were tearing the country apart, the new democratic government developed and rolled out the *Cruzado* Plan in 1986. The plan created a new currency, the Cruzado, which replaced the old Cruzeiro. The plan also froze prices, wages, rents and mortgage payments in order to control inflation, and guaranteed wage increases that would keep up with the consumer price index, which virtually guaranteed continued inflation. Conditions improved for the average Brazilian rather quickly. With higher wages and lower prices on everyday commodities, Brazilians were happy. The price freeze was critical to making the plan work, but also guaranteed that the plan would eventually fail because it also led to overconsumption, near-zero investment, massive capital flight and wide-ranging skepticism among many investors and economists (Roett 2011). The *Cruzado* Plan was announced in February 1986 but by the time elections were over in November of that year, the problems the plan had created were quite prominent (Bresser-Pereira 2009). The government announced a new plan almost immediately after the elections ended, with the clever name *Cruzado* II.

The *Cruzado* II realigned prices on middle-class consumer goods and increased taxes on those goods. The objective was to reduce consumption and encourage saving and investment. The outcome, however, was to simply divert expenditures to substitute goods. Inflation ensued shortly thereafter. By February 1987 the Central Bank of Brazil announced a moratorium on existing debt obligations because its reserves had been depleted (Gordon 2001). This, of course, killed any investor confidence that might have remained up to that point. Brazil's private capital account hit an all-time low, with a deficit of about $10 billion in 1989 (Goldfajn and Minella 2007).

The next set of policies was the Bresser Plan, which failed almost from the beginning. With inflation at 81% per month by March 1990, and GDP growth barely over 1%, something needed to be done. The Bresser Plan adopted new price and wage caps and removed the mechanism that forced wage increases. Due in part to fiscal irresponsibility, and in part to the new constitution of 1988 which transferred a great deal of power and resources from the federal government to the states, the Bresser Plan went the way of its predecessors (Roett 2011). As did the subsequent plan, the *Cruzado Novo* (or New Cruzado), which was a cheap copy of the previous plans but with new price and wage caps and another new currency, the Cruzeiro—the fourth currency in four years and the eighth since 1940 (Novelli and Galvão 2001; Rohter 2012). By this time the Brazilian public was so frustrated and angry with Brasilia that President Sarney rarely left the capital, and relied on a military escort to ensure his personal safety at all times (Roett 2011). Those who supported the democratic transition of 1985 must have begun to reconsider (Gordon 2001). Those who had supported the transition were having their legs cut out from under them by the abysmal economic performance. The economy under the military regime, as bad as it had been, was still better than what the democratically elected government had produced in nearly five years. The national poverty rate in 1990 was well over 40%, with no relief in sight.

Fernando Collor de Mello, who was the first directly elected president of the new regime, took office in 1990. He initiated a broad liberalization program which set the stage for later developments. He created the Collor plan, which confiscated savings and investments to try and stabilize the economy. The plan was unsuccessful and he was impeached in 1992 for corruption (D'Alva Kinzo and Dunkerly 2003). Mello's vice president, Itamar Franco, took over until the next election, in 1994. Franco appointed Fernando Cardoso as finance minister, who then introduced the Plano Real. This plan included another new currency, but also liberalized the economy and weakened state monopolies. This created the stability the economy needed to draw in new investments and growth ensued, though income equality and poverty reduction did not immediately follow (Bresser-Pereira 2002; Rohter 2012).

Cardoso declared the "end of the Vargas Era" in 1994, indicating that Brazil was following sound and sustainable liberal economic principles and abandoning ISI (Novelli and Galvão 2001). As president from 1994 to 2002,

Cardoso was able to get the country through several trying years, which included abandoning a key part of the Real Plan, the currency peg, as well as an IMF package to underpin the Real. Improvements in the economy initially benefited the wealthy, but the poorer classes continued to suffer greatly during this time from the lingering effects of decades of economic turmoil (Baer 2001). So although the economy was beginning to look healthier from the macro perspective, with consistent positive growth, improving trade relationships, acceptable levels of inflation and so on, a large portion of the population was still very dissatisfied. The Plano Real, however, is really what put Brazil on track to later be included with Russia, India and China when Jim O'Neill coined the term BRICs for the four middle-income countries that have the capability of dramatically changing the global economy in the coming decades (O'Neill 2012; Rohter 2012). Finally, with the economy stabilizing in the late 1990s, Cardoso initiated programs that were designed to directly address the needs of the poor, such as the bolsa escola; he simply did not have enough time to get them off the ground before the 2002 election cycle.

From the 1960s up to this point real interest rates had been very high, often upwards of 25%, and at times as high as 65% (Segura-Ubiergo 2012). These high interest rates were almost certainly a result of the inflation that plagued Brazil over the decades. When inflation is high interest rates must also be high in order to stay ahead of inflation. If not, creditors would lose money every time they lent. However, the high interest rates meant that it was rather costly to borrow money. Large enterprises, such as those created and grown through ISI policies, were often able to borrow internationally at much lower rates, but small and medium enterprises, as well as households, generally did not have that option. The steep price of credit put it out of reach for most microentrepreneurs and households. So when microfinance was introduced it met a tremendous, long-standing, unfulfilled demand for credit that was accessible to small actors (Chaves 2011; Mezzera 2002).

Luiz Inácio "Lula" da Silva, or just Lula, campaigned explicitly on the persistent poverty that plagued much of Brazil (Rohter 2012). Lula began his political career in labor unions. He formed the Worker's Party (PT) shortly after the military government authorized political parties in the mid-1970s. He ran for president three times before he was elected in 2002. Lula's and his party's key issues were poverty eradication and rolling back the neoliberal economic policies that many believed had added to the burden of the poor. He even went so far as to say that as president he would not pay Brazil's foreign debts until the Brazilian people were taken care of.[1] His rhetoric made investors and creditors very nervous during the runup to the 2002 election cycle, but because so many Brazilians had been suffering economically for so long Lula won solidly in the run-off election. In the final weeks of the campaign, however, Lula alienated some of the fringe of his party in order to move more towards the center on economic policy. Once in office his fiscal policies were so conservative, especially compared to his campaign rhetoric, that many began calling it Cardoso's third term (Roett 2011).

Lula did begin some of his promised reforms right away though. For example, the Bolsa Escola, which was already in place in 2003, was a Conditional Cash Transfer (CCT) program. Lula merged it with the Bolsa Família to create a national CCT program that would help more than 11 million Brazilians by 2009 (Soares, Ribas, and Osório 2010). The economy settled down to a steadier growth rate, inflation was within an acceptable range of about 3–8% and investment was flowing into Brazil. By 2008 Brazil was given investment grade status on its foreign debt, one of only 14 sovereign states worldwide to receive such a high rating (Roett 2011). In 2010 Brazil had the fourth largest stock market in the world and three of the 10 largest banks in the world, in terms of market capitalization. It also had a booming energy sector, and was growing its industrial and agricultural production.

## MICROFINANCE IN BRAZIL

While all of this was occurring, microfinance efforts spread throughout Brazil. There were programs to make small loans to microentrepreneurs as early as 1973, though the programs were relatively small and isolated (Mota Lopes and Macedo 2012; Meagher et al. 2006). The long history of poverty and inequality for many Brazilians almost certainly made them eager to embrace anything that would help them break out of that cycle. Commercial microfinance made its way to Brazil during the late 1980s and early 1990s. By the late 1990s microfinance was still small, but expanding rather quickly to offer many different products and services to millions of Brazilians (Mandelli 2013; Schonberger 2001). A household's ability to break loose from the shackles of poverty, however, was influenced by turbulence in government bureaucracy and economic policies, as described in the following pages.

An important element of the economic growth model during the late 1990s and early 2000s was the result of a need to attract foreign financing to cover Brazil's external payment imbalances (Medialdea 2013). The government raised interest rates to deter domestic borrowing and attract foreign investment. While this strategy had the intended effect, the unintended effects were that many Brazilians found it nearly impossible to access credit. Only 10% of small and medium enterprises were able to obtain the bank loans they applied for in 1999 (Medialdea 2013, 431). This then led to decreased consumption, salaries and employment. One of the unintended consequences of this policy was the creation of a large, unmet demand for consumer credit and micro, small and medium enterprise credit.

## The First Phase of Microfinance

Many experts expected microfinance to play a major role in Brazil because it seemed that all of the conditions were right for the microfinance industry to flourish; from a growing economy, to high inequality, a liberalizing market, and a commercialized banking sector (Chaves 2011; Nichter, Goldmark, and Fiori 2002; Vanroose 2010). Brazil had rural credit programs and institutions that did some of the same things as MFIs from as early as the 1970s, but the programs were quite limited in their reach and scope. In 1998, no microfinance program had more than a few thousand borrowers and none of them were sustainable programs (Christen, Schonberger, and Roseberg 2004). Microfinance began to grow in Brazil during the late 1990s and early 2000s as it grew in popularity in development circles. In fact, microfinance grew very quickly for a few years after the MFI CrediAmigo was established in 1997. By the end of its first full year it had as many customers as all other MFIs in Brazil combined, and by 2001 it had reached more than 85,000 active borrowers in a country of approximately 177 million, according to World Bank figures (Meagher et al. 2006). CrediAmigo served the Northeast of Brazil, where poverty was especially high. In fact, while the national poverty rate in 1999 was just over 35%, the poverty rate in the northeastern states was generally over 60% with Piauí the highest at over 66%. The microfinance industry grew primarily in the Northeast, with the notable exception of the state of Santa Catarina in the South, which also saw significant microfinance growth from early on. However, this still meant that by 2003, there were fewer than 370,000 borrowers, less than two borrowers per thousand population in a country where more than a quarter of the population lived on less than $2.50 per day.

Figure 5.1 shows that the effect of microfinance is difficult to discern for Brazil as a whole. This is likely because so few Brazilians were able to actually take advantage of microfinancial services in the early years (Chaves 2011; Vanroose 2010). Even in the states with the highest concentrations of microfinance borrowers, only about 0.8% of the population was taking advantage of microfinance at any given time. Often it was far less than that. So, while microfinance might have a significant impact on individual borrowers, it had a limited impact at the national scale. Consequently, there is no obvious relationship between the number of microfinance borrowers in Brazil and infant mortality rates over time. This may also be because infant mortality can be affected by other factors, such as advancements in technology and medical expertise, though they tend to advance at a relatively steady and predictable

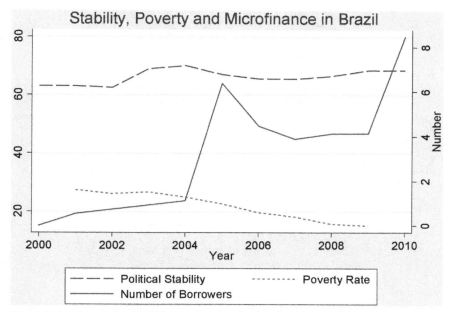

**Figure 5.1. Comparing Stability, Poverty, and Microfinance Trends**

pace.[2] Nor is it immediately apparent that microfinance reduces poverty rates, for many of the same reasons. Looking at the national level of risk in figure 5.2 does not help either. It would be difficult to convince anybody, based on this evidence, either that microfinance matters or that it is interacting with risk.

Constraints on credit, taken together with the high poverty rate in the Northeast and an improving economy and government, seemed like the perfect conditions for microfinance to do its work in the late 1990s and early 2000s. However, the national poverty rate remained nearly stagnant during that time, fluctuating between 33.9% in 1997 and 35.79% in 2003. There was significant variation across states though. The poverty rate for many states increased during this time, likely as a result of the credit crunch, frozen wages and high unemployment (Medialdea 2013). Most states in the Southeast and South saw stagnant or mildly increased poverty rates from 1997 to 2003. No other state in the South or Southeast saw poverty increase as much as São Paulo did though, rising from about 16% to 21.6%, although several of the Northern states saw similar increases. Roraima, for example, a relatively small state sandwiched between Amazonas state, Venezuela and Guyana, saw poverty rates increase from just under 27% in 1997 to about 48% in 2002. In the Northeast, however, where CrediAmigo served more than 80,000 customers, poverty rates neither stagnated nor increased.

Figure 5.2. Map of Brazil (Map creator: Marco Aurelio P. Marsitch. Public Domain. Retrieved from https://commons.wikimedia.org/wiki/File:States_and_Great_Regions_in_Brazil.png, July 31, 2015. Modified by Brian Warby)

The poverty rate in Piauí dropped from 70.1% in 1997 to 61.8% in 2003, which reduced the proportion of the population living in poverty by 12%, and in Maranhão it dropped from 72.5% to 65.9%, which reduced the proportion of people living in poverty by 9%. For additional context, consider table 5.1. The level of microfinance varied considerably across regions. In the Southeast, for example, there were only 1,577 total reported microfinance borrowers in 2003, which meant that there were about .02 borrowers per thousand population.[3] There, poverty rates increased on average. However, the Northeast had around 345,000 borrowers for a rate of about 7 borrowers per thousand residents. The South was somewhere in between with just less than one borrower per thousand residents and poverty rates declined in all three southern states, though not by margins quite as large as in Piauí.[4]

**Table 5.1. Changes in the Number of Borrowers by Region**

|  |  |  | 2003 |  |  |
|---|---|---|---|---|---|
|  | Borrowers | Population | Microfinance/ 1,000 Pop |  |  |
| North | — | 13,504,599 |  |  |  |
| Northeast | 345,274 | 48,845,112 | 7.069 |  |  |
| South | 21,818 | 25,734,253 | 0.848 |  |  |
| Southeast | 1,577 | 74,447,456 | 0.021 |  |  |
|  |  |  | 2009 |  |  |
|  | Borrowers | Population | Microfinance/ 1,000 Pop | % Growth | % Growth in MF/Pop |
| North | 159 | 15,142,684 | 0.011 | — | — |
| Northeast | 460,839 | 53,088,499 | 8.681 | 33.5 | 22.8 |
| South | 129,042 | 27,497,970 | 4.693 | 491.4 | 453.5 |
| Southeast | 94,955 | 80,187,717 | 1.184 | 5,021.2 | 4,590.2 |

On the other hand, the higher beginning poverty rates in the Northeast may mean that it is easier to reduce poverty by the same margins there, relative to other parts of the country. So, Piauí's reduction in poverty from 70% to 61% means that the proportion of poor in Piauí declined by 11%. Maranhão was not too far behind at 9% and Ceará at 7% reductions, but some of the other Northeastern states saw much smaller reductions and three other states actually experienced increases in poverty. Compare this to the South where Santa Catarina's poverty rate dropped from 21% to 15%, for a proportional decline of 30%. Santa Catarina had less than one-seventh the microfinance penetration of the Northeast, but saw much larger relative reductions in the poverty rate. Even accounting for differences in populations, the South reduced poverty by six times as much as the Northeast, which was still considerably better than the rest of the country. So the two regions with the greatest microfinance penetration also saw the greatest declines in poverty from 1997 to 2003. However, one region, the Northeast, suffers from poor governance, while the other region, the South, is often lauded as having some of the best local governments in the country.

The quality of governance is typically better in some regions than in others. This reaches back into Brazil's early history. As one of the country's primary exports in the early days of the republic, sugar declined from about thirty percent of exports to less than five percent between 1820 and 1900. Sugar was primarily grown in the Northeast, so when the Brazilian sugar industry declined, so did employment for many northeasterners, including thousands of former slaves. Coffee was the next major cash crop, but coffee grew better in the more temperate climates of the South and Southeast. There was ample domestic labor to meet the new, booming demand for Brazilian coffee, but elites and government instead recruited and imported labor primarily from Europe and Japan to work in the coffee industry rather than relocating workers from the Northeast because they were seen as more reliable and better able to contribute to the advancement of the country.[5] Consequently, the economy in the south of the country was booming while the Northeast was suffering from high unemployment, low investment and perpetual poverty. The central government concentrated resources on the economically productive southern regions, paying passages for European immigrants, which perpetuated continued growth while Northeasterners could not afford to move south. The result was that the South and Southeast matured economically, financially and politically far more quickly than did the Northeast or the North.

These effects remain today. According to data from the Economist Intelligence Unit (EIU), the South and Southeast have measurably better governance than does the Northeast. The EIU measures the political environment in each state according to its political stability, which includes support for the state government and its ability to pass and implement laws, as well as the strength of political coalitions; corruption, which measures the number of official reports of public-sector corruption in each state; and quality of the bureaucracy, or its capacity to carry out its designated functions. With just one exception, the South and Southeast universally score in the "good" category on corruption, while the Northeast universally scores in the "moderate" category.[6] The aggregate scores for the regions for the general political environment in 2011 were 66.7 for the Southeast, 65.7 for the South, but only 45.4 for the Northeast. The political environment in the southern regions is more conducive to microfinance effectiveness than that in the Northeast. This may have contributed to the better poverty alleviation outcomes observed in the southern regions relative to the Northeast.

Further evidence of the higher quality of governance in the South and Southeast lies in the sub-federal institutions created to foster economic development. The most common form for these institutions to take is an *Agência de Fomento*, which is a non-banking financial institution that advances economic development by supporting micro, small and medium enterprises through accessible credit and help with funding development projects (Dutra 2014). Of the sixteen states with an *Agência de Fomento*, all three of the states in the South have one, and two of the four in the Southeast have one, but the other two have development banks. In the Northeast, only five of the eight states have similar institutions. The other three have nothing of the sort.

The difference in the quality and effectiveness of the government in the Northeast versus that in the Southeast and South is significant. Although the Northeast received far more microfinance relative to the number of people and to incomes, the greatest gains in poverty rates occurred in the South and the greatest gains in educational achievement were in the South and Southeast. The more effective, less corrupt governments of the southern regions compared to the Northeast likely contributed to the better outcomes there.

So, while the Northeast experienced unexpectedly large reductions in poverty during this time frame compared to the rest of the country, those changes might have been even stronger in the presence of better government institutions. The Southern states had the benefit of better governance and generally saw similar reductions in poverty to the Northeast. The major exception to that was Santa Catarina, which had more microfinance and more poverty reduction than any other state. Country-level governance scores put Brazil in the moderately stable category. However, the poorer-than-average governance in the Northeast means that, disaggregated, the region is on the low end of the moderate category, while the southeastern states, with their better-than-average governance, were at the high end of the category. The cross-sectional data seems to support the hypothesis that better government institutions support and strengthen the poverty alleviation effect of microfinance.

## *Alternative Explanations*

There are at least two other potential explanations for the reduction in poverty experienced by the northeastern states during this time that should be acknowledged though. First, it could be the result of government poverty alleviation programs, specifically the CCT programs that were implemented nationally in 2001. Second is education. Education was improving radically, which led to declining illiteracy rates, though the Northeast experienced the greatest gains in literacy. On the other hand, the conditions surrounding these two phenomena cast some doubt on their influence on poverty.

Although Bolsa Família was not launched until 2003, its predecessor programs had already been in place for several years. Bolsa Escola, a CCT program that focused on improving school attendance for children, began as pilot programs in the mid-1990s and was nationally adopted in 2001. CCTs are regarded by many experts as an effective tool for poverty alleviation. They have been attributed with improving school enrollment (Glewwe and Kassouf 2012), reducing stunting typically caused by malnutrition (Fernald, Gertler, and Neufeld 2008), improving maternal and child health (Rasella et al. 2013), reducing teen pregnancy (Baird, McIntosh, and Özler 2011), and more. Brazil's various CCT programs have almost certainly contributed to declining poverty in the country over the last twenty years and by 2003, Bolsa Escola had spread to virtually every municipality in Brazil, though with varying levels of uptake. In some municipalities the number of enrolled families, compared to the projected number of eligible families based on census data, was extremely low. The program was administered at the municipal level and not all municipalities implemented the program with the same vigor. In Utinga Bahia, in the Northeast, for example, enrollment was 0.53% of the number of families census data had predicted would be eligible. However, some municipalities experienced 100% uptake.

On the other hand, the Northeast is comparable to the rest of the country in terms of CCT uptake. The average uptake in the Northeast was about 64% in 2004, compared to a bit under 50% in the North and Central West, 62% in the Southeast and 72% in the South. So initial uptake in the Northeast was most comparable to the Southeast, but microfinance was considerably more common in the Northeast, which may have led to larger decreases in poverty in the Northeast compared to the Southeast.

Brazil was also making tremendous progress in primary and secondary education during this time. The national illiteracy rate for people fifteen and older was over 20% until the late 1980s. However, from the late 1980s to the early 2000s, illiteracy was cut nearly in half, with just 11.6% of the population still illiterate in 2003. The Northeast benefited the most from the push to eliminate illiteracy though. Illiteracy was a problem across all of Brazil, but was particularly prominent in the Northeast, with half of northeastern states at more than 40% illiteracy. Piauí was the highest at 47%. The Northeast made the greatest gains in literacy though; Maranhão, for example, went from 44% illiteracy to less than 24% in the same time frame. The northeastern states accounted for seven of the top eight improvements in literacy during this time period.

To be fair, though, although the Northeast made the greatest marginal gains in reducing illiteracy, relative change was greater in the South than in any other region, which reduced illiteracy by 29% compared to the Northeast's 21% reduction. In fact, in relative terms, the Northeast reduced illiteracy the least. Because illiteracy was high in the Northeast, there was a lot of low-hanging fruit—many people who had the capacity and willingness to improve their educational outcomes and only needed a little more access or a few more resources. In the South, where a much smaller proportion of the population remained illiterate, it likely required greater effort to achieve the same proportional reductions.

Thus far, it appears that microfinance may have some impact on poverty, perhaps in both the Northeast and the South. However, the South certainly saw larger reductions in poverty. Perhaps the greater poverty reduction in the South is a product of stronger relative gains in education, as well as greater uptake of conditional cash transfer programs. The other explanation, though, is that microfinance had a greater impact in the South because the macroconditions were better in the South than in the Northeast.

## The Second Phase of Microfinance

So, while microfinance seems to have reduced poverty, admittedly more in some areas than in others, microfinance has struggled to expand as much in Brazil as it has in some other Latin American countries. Brazil has long had usury laws, which limit interest rates on loans made by anything other than a regulated, commercial bank. The effective cap on interest rates was about 2% per month (Meagher et al. 2006). Banks engaged in micro-lending could charge higher interest rates, but NGO-run MFIs could not. The law was intended to protect the poor from predatory lending practices, but in an industry where 70% APR interest rates are often considered necessary to cover costs, the 2% cap likely discouraged many private investors from entering the market (Aghion and Morduch 2005; Kumar 2005).

During the early 2000s the Brazilian government tried to foster microfinance growth by creating new categories of financial institutions that would allow for commercial MFIs. The legislation package included provisions intended to loosen credit for microfinance by requiring commercial banks to set aside some of their assets to invest in microfinance, but it also discouraged new privately funded lending because it was too difficult to compete with the state-subsidized lenders. The problem became so pronounced that at one point roughly 50% of banks were shirking the legislative requirement to set aside funds for microfinance, opting instead to hold the money in zero interest accounts rather than put the money at risk of default for very modest profits (Meagher et al. 2006). Microfinance did not experience a significant uptick in the growth of the microfinance industry as a result of the legislation, but it did see more types of institutions offering a wider variety of financial services to the poor. Today there are more than 60 MFIs in Brazil, though a significant proportion of them are either government funded or non-profits.

Government involvement in microfinance may have further stunted the industry when the Banco Nacional de Desenvolvimento (National Development Bank), which was supposed to disburse funds to approved MFIs according to a piece of 2003 legislation, failed to do so on time. The late funds caused slow-downs in service among the MFIs (Meagher et al. 2006). This meant that clients did not receive the loans they needed when they expected them. This seemed to reduce loan renewals and, apparently, incentives to repay loans since the default rate subsequently jumped. The difficulties this presented to MFIs were exacerbated by years of continually changing regulations (Chaves 2011). Moreover, most MFIs in Brazil are somewhat limited in the types of services they are legally permitted to provide to their customers. Non-government MFIs are prohibited from accepting deposits and, therefore, deal only in credit. This prevents them from being able to take advantage of some of the innovations that MFIs in other countries use, like tying loans to forced savings accounts, or offering insurance options along with, or even instead, of loans. This same period is also a focal point because Brazil saw a change in risk trends. The environment in Brazil was growing riskier from about 1997 until 2003 (see figure 5.1). After 2004 risk began receding. This was in part due to fluctuations in the value of the Real during the first time period, bouncing from less than R$1/US dollar to well over R$3.5/US dollar from 1996 to 2003. From early 2004 the Real appreciated until in 2008, just before the global recession hit Brazil, the exchange rate was nearly R$1.5/US dollar again. Thanks in part to this consistency, the 2004–2008 time period was a good one for business in Brazil, much better than the 1997–2003 time period.

It is important to look at differences in the growth of microfinance across these regions too. Microfinance increased in every region, but it did not increase evenly across regions. From 2003 to 2008 microfinance grew by only 23% in the Northeast, a rather modest increase considering the growth over the previous five years from nearly zero to more than 345,000 borrowers. In the South it grew by about 450% and in the Southeast it grew by around 4,600%. However, microfinance remained most concentrated in the Northeast, with well over eight borrowers per thousand population, nearly twice as much as in the South, which had less than five borrowers per thousand population. However, the South also had much lower poverty rates, so if microloans were going exclusively to the poor, though that was not strictly the case, there was more market saturation in the South than in the Northeast.[7]

While poverty generally decreased more quickly in the northeastern states than for most other states during 1997–2003 ($T_1$), at least in absolute terms, the reverse is true for 2004–2009 ($T_2$). Recall that during $T_1$, São Paulo saw poverty increase by 34%, but it was nearly cut in half during $T_2$ from 20.58% to 11.01%. Paraná, another southern state, saw poverty decrease from 22.7% to 12.37% for a total reduction in poverty of 46% during the same time period, compared to a mere 14% reduction during $T_1$. Though not as dramatic as the South and Southeast, the northeastern states also saw a jump in poverty reduction during $T_2$. In Piauí, poverty decreased by 12% during $T_1$ and by 36% during $T_2$. For Maranhão the $T_1$ reduction was 9% and $T_2$ reduction was 35%. The differences in the rate of change from $T_1$ to $T_2$ for most of Brazil are dramatic. In São Paulo the rate of reduction swung wildly from a 30% increase to a 50% decrease. In Paraná the swing was 32%, much closer to the national average. In the northeastern states the changes were more modest. In Piauí the swing was only 24% and 25% in Maranhão.

To understand the meaning of these changes in poverty we must keep in mind that there are many conditions that affect poverty, and microfinance is just one of them. Lula's Bolsa Família program was implemented nationally around the beginning of $T_2$, which almost certainly contributed significantly to national poverty reduction. The economy was stronger and more stable, so businesses grew. Official unemployment shrank from over 12% to under 8%. Wages, instead of shrinking, began to grow again. GDP per capita PPP (purchasing power parity) grew from less than \$8,000 at the beginning of 2004 to more than \$9,500 in 2009.

There were a lot of reasons for poverty to decrease during $T_2$, but the fact remains that it decreased considerably in regions where microfinance was growing the fastest. The South and Southeast saw some of the greatest reductions in poverty rates, in some cases cutting poverty by nearly sixty percent. Despite the growth of microfinance in the South and Southeast during $T_2$, it remained more intensive in the Northeast than anywhere else in the country. This seems to suggest that microfinance can have an impact, but the impact appears to be much greater when government institutions also promote poverty alleviation. Unfortunately, the poorer quality of governance in the Northeast may have prevented microfinance from having as much impact on poverty as it seems to have had in the South and Southeast.

## RATIONAL PEASANTS IN BRAZIL

The beginning of this chapter started by discussing the findings of the previous chapter and pointing out that because risk increases uncertainty about the future, potential clients should be wary of undertaking ventures, such as microloans, when risk is high because it could lead to financial problems down the road when loan payments are due. If a potential client does not pursue a microloan because risk is high and the future is uncertain, though she cannot improve her quality of life through microfinance, she might be avoiding possible future financial ruin. Samuel Popkin's research on the financial lives of peasants foreshadowed these results. Popkin's Rational Peasant argument (1979) is that peasants continually make efforts to improve their quality of life through long- and short-term public and private investments (Popkin 1979, 413). This clearly fits well with microfinance since it provides peasants the opportunity to pursue short- and medium-term private investments. Many peasants might not be able to secure themselves against risk of severely damaging loss when uncertainty is high, but if they can under better conditions, and they foresee the possibility of "measurably improving their position," they are likely to accept the risk (Popkin 1979, 425). Popkin would predict that we should see peasants acting rationally, making calculated decisions that will maximize their financial options. When the conditions are right they will take advantage of microfinance to the extent that it is useful.

The Brazilian constitution of 1988 strengthened local governments, giving them more autonomy and resources in order to make decisions based on the needs of their own people. Most of these states existed before 1988, and there was considerable variation between them in terms of the nature and health of their economies, bureaucracy and level of human development. The new constitution gave states the power to develop unique approaches based on their individual situations. Although each state has the autonomy to develop unique policies, and they often do, there are similarities within each region. The data produced by the EIU discussed above illustrates the disparities across the country. Each region is given a score from 0 to 100, where 100 represents the best possible environment. For the productivity of labor the Southeast scored 81.3 while the Northeast scored 19.4. For the number of university graduates per capita, the Southeast scored 87.5, while the Northeast scored 36.1 and the North 10.7. When it comes to corruption, the South scored 50 while the Northeast scored only 25, the North only 21.4 and the Central West only 18.8. Turning to demographics, São Paulo alone accounted for more than 40% of GNP and more than 25% of national population in 1995 (Selcher 1998). The poverty rates in 2010 range from a high of 60.45% in Alagoas, a northeastern state, to a low of 10.5 in Santa Catarina, a southern state (IBGE). Although there are some regions in the North with very high poverty rates, the Northeast generally gets the most attention in discussions of poverty reduction for two reasons. First, the Northeast has consistently high poverty across the region and has had since the Brazilian sugar industry collapsed in the middle of the nineteenth century (Meade 2010). Second, the Northeast has a drastically higher population density than the North, the other high poverty region, which means there are more poor people in the Northeast who need help than there are in the North.

Not surprisingly, Northeastern states consistently rank among the worst for political environment and are the nine lowest ranked states for economic environment according to the data just mentioned. Nonetheless, microfinance flourishes in the Northeast. Most of the first MFIs in Brazil, such as Credi-Amigo, began in the Northeast and have survived the economic and political turmoil the country has experienced over the years. Every northeastern state has more MFI clients per capita than any other state.[8] The state with the highest value in loans per capita is Piauí, which competes with Alagoas for the title of poorest state in the union. In fact, with one exception, every northeastern state has a higher loan value per capita figure than any other state in the union despite the repressed economy in that region.[9] Moreover, the size of the average loan in the Northeast is comparable to loans in other parts of the country, once the cost of living is accounted for.

To be fair, receipt of loans does not necessarily mean that the loans are being used productively. There are two obvious ways to figure out if loans are being used productively. The first and most straightforward is to track it directly either by asking borrowers what they are doing with their loans and how the loans are affecting their finances and following their financial transactions the way Collins et al. (2009) did. This is a highly resource intensive approach. The second method, which is slightly less precise but far more cost effective, is to infer it from the aggregated data. Assuming that repayment rates are a reasonable proxy for the borrowers' finances after taking the loan provides a picture of how productive the loans are. The logic behind this inference is that a borrower who used the loan money productively would be able to repay the loan easily since she has more money coming in than she had before. A borrower who did not use the loan productively, on the other hand, might find it difficult to repay the loan since she has no more money coming in than before, but has an additional expense. Not all of these unproductive borrowers are going to default, but those who do default are almost certainly unable to improve their incomes by any significant margin and are likely worse off as a result of the loan. So states or regions with higher default rates can be assumed to have a less productive microfinance sector.

As an example of what a productive borrower might look like, a study of the Brazilian MFI CEAPE-PB (Center for Support of Small Enterprises—in Paraíba) found that 88% of its customers in 2004 reportedly operated in the commercial sector, 8% in production and 4% in the service sector (Pereira 2005). Among those operating in the commercial sector, 70% sold clothing. Selling clothes is likely an attractive option for many microentrepreneurs because it requires relatively little capital to get started. At the lowest end of the spectrum, some microentrepreneurs have carts they park on street corners from which they might sell shorts, T-shirts and dresses. Several sets of these in three or four sizes might be all a microentrepreneur needs to get started. She can buy more stock as needed with the proceeds from previous sales. Alternatively, virtually every Brazilian city has an open-air market. Vendors are generally required to pay a minor fee for the privilege of setting up shop in the market, but the market is often the primary shopping area for customers who do not want to pay higher prices for name-brand clothes at traditional retail outlets. The vendor who starts off by selling T-shirts from her cart on the street corner might take a loan to expand her stock, buying larger quantities for lower marginal prices, and thereby capturing more profits. The microentrepreneur might continue to expand by increasing the types of goods she sells, or by renting a booth in the local market. She might even eventually open a small shop of her own. With each step up the commercial ladder the microentrepreneur might need a loan to make the jump. Once she has made the jump, her earning potential increases. On the other hand, if she takes a loan and makes a bad business choice, she might not have any more profit than before, or might even reduce her profits, but she has an additional expense in the loan repayments of principal plus interest.

So the average percentage of the loan portfolio with payment delays of 90 days or greater and, therefore, by common definition at risk of default, tells an important story. When the loan portfolio at risk is weighted by the number of borrowers, the region with the lowest default rate in 2009 was the Southeast at 2.15%.[10] Next was the Northeast with a weighted default rate of 3.41%. Last was the South, which is dominated by Santa Catarina, the one state that compares to the Northeast in terms of microfinance saturation, at 3.67%. The implication is that borrowers in the Northeast are just as good at using micro-loans as people in other regions of the country. In fact, accepting the assumption above, there is a broader conclusion from the data. Microfinance borrowers are better than average borrowers at using loans productively considering that the national rate of payment delays of 90 days or more for personal credit is consistently over 5.5%, according to the Brazilian Central Bank (bcb.gov. br). Peasants appear to be quite capable of taking risks and making productive investments, at least when government institutions are functioning well.

## CONCLUSION

This chapter examines the industrial and economic development in Brazil from 1930 to the present, paying particular attention to the role of the state in the development process. Over the past 80 years Brazil has seen periods of significant growth and periods of suffocating stagnation, debt and poverty. With that background, two distinct periods in the development of Brazilian microfinance are compared. The first period, 1997–2003, was a period of uncertainty and generally modest economic performance for the country. In the Northeast and other states where microfinance was primarily concentrated at the time, poverty declined much more quickly than in the rest of the country. During the second time period, however, 2004–2009, risk was low, the economy was generally robust and microfinance had spread outside of the Northeast. Other poverty alleviation programs had proliferated as well. While poverty reduction advanced more quickly in the Northeast during the first time period, it advanced more slowly there than in the rest of the country during the second time period. Nevertheless, microfinance remained more intensive in the Northeast than in any other region.

The implication, relative to this study, is that, as in chapter 4, the empirical evidence supports some facets of the theory from chapter 3. Microfinance appears to have a detectable impact on poverty under some conditions, but not others, and political stability seems to strengthen that impact. The evidence is convincing, if not entirely conclusive. The end result is that this examination of how microfinance and political and economic risk factors affect poverty rates in Brazil stacks up in favor of the same conclusions arrived at in chapter 4. Microfinance as a poverty alleviation mechanism is indeed sensitive to macro conditions, including political stability.

The final section of this chapter addressed Popkin's rational peasant hypothesis (Popkin 1979). Popkin argued that peasants are rational actors whose primary interest is securing their individual long-term economic well-being. As such, they are capable of, and willing to make, investments and take risks in order to improve their position, despite having very little income. Chapter 4 and chapter 5 both suggest that the poor are indeed capable of making their way out of poverty by taking risks and making investments through microfinance.

## NOTES

1. Lula did not actually follow through with this threat.

2. Recall that in chapter 4, the dependent variable was the rate of change in infant mortality. The models were picking up on variations from the normal, predictable advancements brought about by new technology and knowledge.

3. Microfinance information was not recorded at the state level in Brazil until the government agency PNMPO began tracking it in 2007. This microfinance data comes from theMIX.org, which collects information at the MFI level, not the state level. This makes it impossible to determine precisely how much microfinance there is in each state because many MFIs serve more than one state. Dividing microfinance by region is more manageable though.

4. There are some MFIs that serve multiple regions. Those were excluded from these calculations since it is impossible to know how it was divided among the regions. Since the point of the discussion is to compare across regions and those that operate inter-regionally do not consistently offer more services in one region than another, I do not believe that this biases the results.

5. This was the early Brazilian version of social Darwinism.

6. The one exception to "good" rating in the South and Southeast was Espírito Santo, in the Southeast, which borders the Northeast and consistently suffers from higher corruption than other states in the region. These results were consistent across the three years for which data is available, and across a variety of indicators and subindicators. The pattern was not quite as consistent for the quality of bureaucracy as it was for corruption, for example, but the quality of bureaucracy is higher, on average, in the South and Southeast than in the Northeast, which means that the government is more effective at providing public services in the southern regions. These two, corruption and bureaucracy, are the key areas with which much of Brazil really struggles. Political stability does not vary nearly as much, but inasmuch as it does vary, it is, once again, better on average in the southern regions than in the Northeast.

7. Assuming that all microloans are going to the poor may be a heroic assumption. Recall from chapter 2 that much research has found that microloans often go to the not-so-poor or even middle class, rather than the truly poor.

8. Data on state level microfinance comes from the Brazilian *Programa Nacional de Microcrédito Produtivo Orientado*.

9. The exception is Santa Catarina, which is uniquely saturated with microfinance outside of the Northeast.

10. These default figures may seem low considering these loans are generally made without any collateral, often to the poorest members of society, but they are actually quite normal for microfinance globally (Aghion and Morduch 2005; Dowla and Barua 2006).

## Chapter Six

# Is Funding Going Where
# It Can Do the Most Good?

As microfinance has grown to become a large global industry, the demand for these services is apparent. The World Bank estimates that there are still 2.5 billion financially excluded adults, most of whom live in perpetual poverty (*Microfinance and Financial Inclusion: At a Glance* 2014). Microfinance institutions have popped up around the globe in an effort to meet the demand. This has required the microfinance industry to scale up dramatically, which it has done with reasonable success. There are today thousands of microfinance institutions around the world, reaching nearly 100 million borrowers. However, one of the big questions that still plagues the microfinance revolution is whether it actually helps the poor, or simply lures them into debt traps. Previous chapters have argued that the best answer is, as economists are fond of saying, it depends. Microfinance can help alleviate poverty under the right conditions, but it can also be useless or perhaps even counter-productive under the wrong conditions. The pragmatist is, by now, asking whether microfinance institutions are generally operating in the right places, where microfinance can help the poor, or in the wrong places, where they will exacerbate poverty. This chapter discusses where microfinance is most common and whether the conditions there are conducive to poverty alleviation, as well as a few places where more microfinance might do some good. It also compares microfinance to other poverty alleviation mechanisms to look at some of the opportunity costs of microfinance.

## WHERE DOES THE MONEY COME FROM?

One of the keys to understanding whether microfinance is going to the right places is to understand the financial structure within which most MFIs are

103

operating. People often assume that since microfinance is intended to help the poorest of the population, the industry is provided capital by government programs, NGOs or through aid donations. Those are the actors that most people associate with poverty alleviation efforts, after all. However, while all of these play a role in financing microloans, they are only part of the picture. Many early microfinance programs began with grants from these sources, but they represent relatively limited sources of capital. Governments in developing countries, where there are high concentrations of financially excluded adults and microfinance is in high demand, typically struggle to meet the state's most basic obligations, such as funding education, police forces, and other public services. They might be able to allocate small amounts of money to microfinance, but not enough to fund the scaling up the industry needs to reach billions of financially excluded adults worldwide.

NGOs face similar constraints. They depend on donations for their funds. NGOs must court philanthropists and other interested parties to provide their operation budgets, as well as any capital that they then pass on. Here again, this is part of the financing story, but a relatively small part. In addition to one-time grants, some NGOs also lend money to MFIs at favorable rates. By lending money for little or no interest to the MFI, the MFI can lend-on to the microfinance customer at a higher rate, which covers the MFI's operation costs and the interest due on the NGO's loan. Foreign aid sometimes plays a similar role. While these are great, low-cost sources of capital, they are quite limited and if there were no other options, scaling up microfinance to reach the 2.5 billion financially excluded adults would be rather difficult.

Fortunately, there are other options. One is that MFIs also obtain capital through deposits, the way banks often do. They then use the savings to make loans. However, only a small portion of MFIs are able to raise capital through this route because they are often legally prevented from accepting deposits or because regulations on deposit taking make it onerous and cost-prohibitive (Galema, Lensink, and Spierdijk 2011; Cull, Demirgüç-Kunt, and Morduch 2011). Even where it is relatively easy to accept deposits, customers' deposits are generally so small as to provide only a fraction of the capital needed to fund the MFI. Indeed, CGAP's (Consultative Group to Assist the Poor) annual Funder Survey indicates that deposits are a relatively small part of most MFIs' asset portfolio (El-Zoghbi, Gahwiler, and Lauer 2011).[1]

The inherent limits on the funding sources described so far have led the microfinance industry to move towards commercial loans for capital that they can then lend-on to their customers. Commercial loans are, of course, going to come with higher costs, which are inevitably passed on, to a greater or lesser extent, to customers. But even here there are some obstacles. In the US it is relatively easy to open a bank account. Most any bank would be glad to open a free savings account, perhaps with a modest minimum balance. One can secure a loan with little more than proof of income, and even that is not always a requirement. The US is also flush with capital. The ease with which one can secure a loan is driven, in large part, by the abundance of capital in the economy. Investors are looking for opportunities to collect a return on their capital, so they want to lend their money out if they can be reasonably confident that it will be repaid with interest. In places where consumers find it difficult to access financial services, the same processes are at work, but in the opposite direction. Rather than an abundance of capital making it relatively easy to get a loan, the lack of capital makes it difficult to get a loan. It also means that investors are likely to be very cautious about whom they lend their money to and will charge much higher rates, all else being equal, for borrowers who appear to be higher risk (see chapter 3 for a discussion of risk and return).

The combination of capital shortages in developing countries where the demand for microfinance is greatest, and the difficulty of mobilizing sufficient deposits means that MFIs often must look to commercial lenders, both domestic and foreign, in order to secure their capital needs. Debt accounts for about two thirds of all microfinance funding (Wiesner and Quien 2010). Grants and equity, or interest earned from loans to microfinance customers, each account for roughly 15% of funding. Deposits make up only a small portion of total global microfinance funding. It is also worth noting that more than half of all foreign funding for MFIs is funneled through a few dozen organizations, called Microfinance Investment Vehicles (MIVs), which evaluate MFIs, usually based on their financial performance (Galema, Lensink, and Spierdijk 2011).

A relatively recent phenomenon is the person-to-person lending facilitated by programs such as Kiva.org. These programs allow individuals with capital to lend money to individuals who need capital through a participating MFI. Under Kiva's program the lender lends money at zero interest to the MFI, who lends-on to a microfinance borrower. The borrower gets the loan she needs, the MFI gets to keep the equity from the loan, or interest earned, and the lender gets her principal back once the loan is repaid. It is crowd-sourced microfinance funding. While this is an interesting development, it is still relatively new and accounts for only a tiny fraction of all microfinance funding.

## RIGHT INSTITUTIONS?

Globally, microfinance is being funded on a large scale. CGAP's 2014 funders survey reported more than $29 billion committed to advance financial inclusion for the previous year. But is the money going to the right types of institutions? Simply having a big bankroll is not enough for an MFI to alleviate poverty. In fact, there is some evidence that having a big bankroll may actually impede some MFIs from operating as effectively as they might otherwise. We should be aware of which types of institutions should be receiving the money and compare that to which institutions are actually receiving funding.

One controversial issue in microfinance circles is the debate over whether there is a place for profit-oriented MFIs, which was briefly discussed in chapter 2. On one end of the spectrum are those who argue that it would be immoral to make a profit off the backs of the poorest of the poor by charging high interest rates. For example, some individuals are growing quite wealthy by locking the poor into debt traps with inexcusably high interest rates (Roodman 2012). When MFIs turn to the private sector for financing, they have to pay market rates on the capital they borrow. In order to remain sustainable the MFIs have to pass those higher interest rates on to their customers by charging interest rates high enough to cover the MFI's operating costs as well as the interest on the commercial loan funding their own microloan. Then if the MFI wants to expand operations by increasing its capital through equity, it must charge still higher interest in order to accumulate capital so that it can expand operations. Meanwhile, the poor, the most vulnerable segment of society, those who are least capable of paying those kinds of astronomical interest rates, are left with no other choice. If they want access to loans, which we assume they must have if they wish to invest in their microenterprises or personal well-being, they must pay the inflated interest rates. If they are unwilling to pay the inflated interest rates, then they are left without access to financial services.

On the other hand is the camp that argues that profit-oriented lending is the only way we, as a global society, can hope to make significant gains in financing the poor. It is a matter of scaling up. With nearly one-third of the global population currently financially excluded we must find a way to scale up microfinance quickly. The main body of this camp would agree that grants are the optimal source of funding, but grants are simply too limited (Barry and Tacneng 2014; Maisch, Soria, and Westley 2006; Mersland and Urgeghe 2013). Taking deposits and accumulating equity can play a role as well, but in the end these methods simply do not provide enough capital to continue scaling up microfinance. The only other option is to turn to commercial loans. The global commercial financial market has an enormous supply of capital, somewhere in the neighborhood of $200 trillion just in the global stocks and bonds market, based on typical market figures in 2015. These investors are willing to lend to the right borrower and for the right price. With access to this kind of capital supply, the microfinance industry can continue scaling up in order to meet pent up demand among the poor for financial services. The argument that it makes for usurious interest rates does not seem to carry much weight since microfinance customers appear to be quite willing to pay the high interest rates required to gain access to financial services.

There is a small, but growing, cohort that supports profit-oriented lending who argues that not only is it acceptable and even necessary to turn to commercial finance to fund MFIs, but that it may be more efficient (Ghosh and Van Tassel 2011, 2013). Grants, the argument goes, allow an MFI to operate relatively inefficiently. Since the MFI is not paying interest on the grant money, the institution's sustainability does not depend to a significant degree on how much of the money it lends-on to microfinance customers. It can afford to waste a lot of the grant money on management inefficiency within the institution, creating a sub-optimal outcome for poverty-minimizing donors and for the financially excluded poor. In an atmosphere where MFIs must compete for funds, on the other hand, they operate efficiently and have sound financial structures, lending-on as much of their assets as possible in order to remain sustainable.

The retort, especially from the first camp, is that there are better ways of ensuring that MFIs are accountable. A variety of ratings agencies closely monitor MFIs' finances in order to help donors and investors direct their capital to the types of institutions that are likely to advance their objectives.[2] This method could keep interest rates low while still rewarding both financial and social efficiency. The research shows that there are detectable patterns in the type of funding that each variety of institution is likely to attract. MFIs that focus on their social mission, which typically includes targeting the poorest of the poor and women, are more likely to attract grants and subsidized loans (Annim 2012; Mersland and Urgeghe 2013). These are the borrowers for whom microfinance has the greatest potential impact. Institutions that are more financially sound are more likely to attract commercial financing, but they are also less likely to service the poorest of the poor or to service women (Cull, Demirgüç-Kunt, and Morduch 2009).

What we see is that, first, there are far more non-profit MFIs in Latin America than for-profit MFIs. In 2012, 162 non-profits and 93 for-profits managed to secure funding. However, the for-profits were funded at a much higher level, with an average of nearly US$750,000 per MFI, where the non-profits averaged only US$290,000 each. The non-profits typically pay marginally higher interest rates, but are also given about 30% longer loan terms on average. These trends are fairly consistent across all types of funders and over time.

If we accept the common conclusion that non-profit MFIs are generally more focused on social efficiency and are more likely to target the poor, then it appears that a large portion of microfinance funding is going to the wrong types of MFIs based on the premise that microfinance is supposed to help alleviate poverty. Although the microfinance industry is growing quite rapidly, much of it may be having little impact on poverty, and what impact it does have, is not always good. We begin, now, to see where the microfinance "heretics" who condemn profit-oriented microfinance are coming from (Sinclair 2012). It is difficult to say with certainty how much poverty alleviation impact for-profit MFIs might have compared to non-profits, but the microfinance industry appears to be operating well below optimal efficiency, based on what we know about how different institutional structures affect poverty and the types of institutions that dominate the industry. One part of the difficulty in discussing specific figures is that most analyses focus on the MFIs and their financial records rather than on poverty alleviation. So we know quite a lot about what is good for MFIs, but not nearly as much about what is actually good for the poor. Another part of the problem is that all of this discussion must be couched in the larger context of the macro-level conditions in which these MFIs are operating, which the next section examines.

## RIGHT COUNTRIES?

Previous chapters discussed some of the macro conditions in which microfinance should be most effective. Empirical analyses showed that things like political stability and law and order have an impact on whether microfinance actually alleviates poverty. So, even if the bulk of microfinance funding were going to the right types of institutions, that would be no guarantee that they would actually be affecting poverty the way we might expect. This section takes a deeper look at whether funding is being directed to MFIs in the countries where it is most likely to have a significant impact on poverty.

Based on the analysis in chapter 4, the Latin American country where microfinance is expected to have the greatest impact, all else being equal, was Chile, which is among the most stable, both politically and economically. Actual funding does not reflect what the data suggests would be the optimal allocation of resources. Chile received virtually no foreign funding. Chile's microfinance industry is dominated by large banks whose primary operations are commercial finance, but which also include microfinance services as well (*Global Microscope on the Microfinance Business Environment* 2012). Since these institutions' primary operations are in commercial finance and microfinance is almost an afterthought, they have little need to court funding from the same sources that other MFIs often turn to. According to data from the MIX, in all of Chile, from 2007 to the present, the entire microfinance industry has acquired about US$ 26.6 million in foreign funding. This figure may seem large at first blush, but tiny El Salvador, with a GDP of one tenth and a population of just more than one third of Chile's, received four times that amount in 2012 alone. In fact, Haiti, with its economy still in tatters and GDP per capita about one-twentieth of Chile's, received twenty percent more funding in 2012 than Chile has received in total since 2007.

To be fair, Chile's microfinance industry being dominated by commercial banks makes it somewhat different from most other Latin American countries because it has less need for foreign funding, so it is useful to look at other cases. After Chile, Mexico, Panama and Costa Rica are all about equally well situated to benefit from microfinance. Costa Rica, the country with the second best political conditions for microfinance effectiveness, received over US$ 40 million in the same year. Nevertheless, as a proportion of GDP per capita, which gives us a sense of market saturation or the marginal impact of another dollar, it was fifteenth out of seventeen countries for which data was available. With its relatively stable political situation and strong law and order, it received less funding in relative terms than El Salvador, Haiti, the Dominican Republic and Jamaica. Panama and Uruguay, states that are consistently politically stable, but in which law and order is not as robust as in Chile, also received negligible or no foreign funding. However, Mexico, which is similar to Panama and Uruguay in its macro conditions, was one of the top five recipients of foreign microfinance funding. Still, it is not clear that political stability has much impact on funding decisions.

As discussed in chapter 4, Chile and Costa Rica had relatively low poverty rates, so these outcomes may not seem all that surprising. After all, if we assume that microfinance is intended to help alleviate poverty, there would be less need for it in a country where poverty is already relatively low, such as Chile with only about 11% of the population living on less than $2.50 per day, or Uruguay, with only 5% at the same poverty level. On the other hand, Panama's poverty rate was about 25% compared to Peru's rate of 28%, but Peru received more than 420 times as much foreign funding, in relative terms. Peru's microfinance industry is far more developed than Panama's, so it is more capable of absorbing that kind of funding, but this does not change the fact that the macro environment in Panama is more conducive to poverty alleviation via microfinance than in Peru. Mexico's poverty rate, on the other hand, is significantly lower than Panama's at 17%. In fact, Mexico has the next lowest poverty rate after Chile. On the other hand, Mexico receives more foreign funding than Nicaragua, with its poverty rate of 44% or Honduras, which has a poverty rate of 50%.

Looking at poverty through the lens of infant mortality (chapter 4), rather than poverty head count at $2.50 per day, does not change the story much.

Chile, Costa Rica and Uruguay have the three lowest infant mortality rates, with Mexico in sixth place and Panama in tenth out of twenty. Nevertheless, Panama has a higher infant mortality at 17.2 than Peru at 14.9, but receives only a fraction of the funding that Peru receives. So, it is difficult to say that poverty alleviation is the driving force behind microfinance funding. Instead, investors appear to be focused on the financial record of the MFIs in which they are investing, regardless of their impact on poverty.

## A Look at Ecuador

Ecuador has been among the most politically unstable countries in Latin America for many years. A brief look at the country's history and the current president's political record will illustrate some of the reasons for its consistently low stability. Ecuador is ethnically and geographically divided by the Andes Mountains. The western, coastal side is peopled primarily by European and African descendants while the highlands are populated primarily by indigenous peoples. Racial divisions have long been at the roots of political conflicts in the country. Also, political parties are highly regional and often tied to individuals rather than clear and specific platforms, which means they come and go at short intervals (Weeks 2015). Moreover, oil has been a major component of Ecuador's national economy since the early 1970s. As with other states that rely heavily on oil, the economy is prone to waves of dramatic expansion and contraction, depending on the global price of oil.

Rafael Correa won the presidential election of 2006 and took office in 2007. Correa represented a shift to the left in Ecuadorian politics, at least on most issues. Correa came into office as a "proponent of 'twenty-first-century socialism'" (Skidmore, Smith, and Green 2014). Correa was trained as an economist at the University of Illinois, where he wrote his dissertation on the negative effects of liberal economic policies in Latin America. As president he quickly began reversing some of the liberal economic policies that he saw as particularly damaging to the country (Andrade and North 2011). He also managed to get a new constitution passed in 2008, which, among other things, allowed him to run for another term in office and concentrated more power in the hands of the executive. Subsequent referenda further concentrated power in the executive, making him remarkably powerful. The 2009 election was closer than in 2006, but Correa won a second term in office and continued his push to the left. He has since secured yet another election victory and will remain in office until at least 2017.

Correa depended on oil revenue to fund his popular social spending programs. The global recession of 2008–2009 decreased those revenues, which forced him to make up the difference elsewhere. One measure that Correa enacted was to scrap police bonuses. This led to protests by police who fired tear gas at Correa, leaving him trapped in a hospital for more than twelve hours, and was accompanied by looting and occupation of several government buildings (BBC News 2010). He declared this incident an attempted coup and declared a state of emergency in which he mobilized military forces to disperse the protesters.

In the meantime, Correa's policies frayed political and economic relations with the US. He terminated free-trade talks with the Bush administration. He refused to pay off Ecuador's foreign debt without restructuring. He formed or strengthened political and economic alliances with leftist regimes in Bolivia, Venezuela, and China. Correa also broke off relations with Colombia in 2008 after Colombian forces attacked a FARC (Fuerzas Armadas Revolucionários de Colombia) stronghold in Ecuadorian territory.

Despite all of this, Ecuador receives relatively large amounts of foreign microfinance funding. As a proportion of GDP/capita, Ecuador was among the top five recipients of foreign funding in 2011–2012. Admittedly, the economy is not very large, with a GDP of about US$ 70 billion in 2010, and the people are not very wealthy, with GDP per capita at about US$4,600. The political situation does not seem to matter all that much to microfinance investors, as evidenced by the lack of correlation between political stability and funding shown in figure 6.1. This is, perhaps, not surprising since little attention has

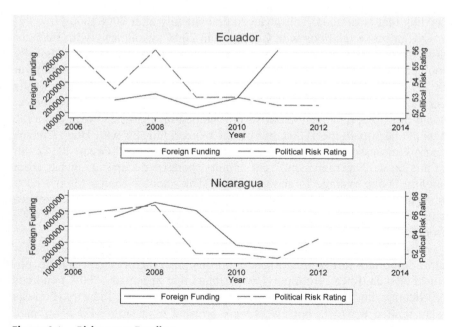

Figure 6.1.    Risk versus Funding

been given to the link between political stability and microfinance impact, but it has significant implications for the impact of the industry as a whole.

## A Look at Nicaragua

Nicaragua serves as a counter-example to Ecuador. Nicaragua has been rated above average in political stability since the mid-1990s. It peaked in 2008, shortly after Daniel Ortega won the presidency in 2006 on the Sandinista ticket. Ortega, much like Correa, embarked on a social spending spree (Vanden and Prevost 2015). Ortega was also less than friendly with the US, although, unlike Correa, Ortega maintained a working relationship with the US, even cooperating on free-trade talks. Ortega also fostered relationships with his neighbors and with China, which proposed a "Great Canal" project across Nicaragua that is, as of this writing, under consideration by Chinese investors and the Nicaraguan government.

In 2008, Nicaragua was the top recipient of foreign funding for microfinance in all of Latin America, relative to GDP per capita, higher even than Peru or Bolivia, which tend to dominate microfinance in Latin America. This is in part because Nicaragua is also one of Latin America's poorest states. GDP per capita is quite low; less than US$1,500 per person in 2008. However, even in absolute terms, only Peru, Mexico and Bolivia received more funding that Nicaragua. This changed dramatically after 2008 though.

Ortega broke relations with Colombia in 2008 in solidarity with Ecuador after the Colombian incursion of Ecuadorian territory. He also successfully lobbied the Supreme Court to rule that he could run for an additional term in 2011, which he won. Many critics have argued against the legality of the decision (Weeks 2015). Ortega has also been accused of harassing and, in some cases, imprisoning journalists on trumped-up charges. Ortega is not the Marxist he was in the 1980s, but he has aligned himself with Hugo Chávez and his successor, Nicolás Maduro (Skidmore, Smith, and Green 2014). All of this caused Nicaraguan political stability scores to decline somewhat, from slightly above average to about average. This modest change should have little or no impact on microfinance effectiveness, but it strongly correlates with levels of foreign funding for Nicaraguan MFIs, which dropped by 65% from 2008 to 2011.

However, there was something else happening in early 2009, something far more important to the microfinance industry than the president and his political agenda. Recall from previous chapters that in January 2009, hundreds of Nicaraguans began protesting against the microfinance industry. Protests were ignited when six borrowers were arrested by a large MFI for unpaid loans (Pachico 2009). Their families protested in the streets and popular discontent spread the protests around the country. What began as protests evolved into a movement that would come to be known as the *"No Pago!"* (I won't pay) movement. By mid-2009 Ortega was addressing the No Pago protesters in his speeches, but rather than urge them toward caution and level-headedness, the left-leaning president condoned and even encouraged them to rebel against the "loan sharks" (Bedecarrats, Bastiaensen, and Doligez 2012). His support for No Pago helped Ortega paint himself as an executive who was in touch with the common people and who would fight for their interests. The Ortega government continued to sympathize and benefit from the No Pago movement until its supporters turned violent, which resulted in several casualties (Campion, Ekka, and Wenner 2010). The movement largely fizzled out after the government introduced legislation on debt forgiveness, but not before some MFIs closed operations in Nicaragua and foreign investors clamped down on funding for Nicaraguan MFIs. The apparent correlation between political risk and microfinance funding for Nicaragua is likely spurious. It was not a dramatic change in political or economic risk that brought about the reduction in funding, it was investors' concerns that they would lose their money if the microfinance crisis in Nicaragua continued. Investors did not care about political risk. They were concerned that MFIs would become insolvent and unable to repay their commercial and institutional lenders.

## Regressions

Regression analysis shows that political stability does not have a statistically significant impact on funding in a one-tailed test. Levels of microfinance funding tend to be relatively trenchant. Some states receive far more, and other states far less, funding than the level of poverty, GDP per capita, or a variety of other measures would suggest. Political stability does not seem to have any significant impact on the general level of foreign funding. Nor do poverty, or the number of borrowers in a country appear to affect the level of funding. From the data, it does not look like poverty alleviation is a concern for investors at all.

Within those trenchant cross-sectional trends at the country level are annual variations in funding. The skeptic might argue that the general level of funding might not be sensitive to political stability, but the level of funding within a country from year to year could be. It is possible that the rough level of funding over time is dependent on financial characteristics that prevail in a given state, but that the year-to-year changes in funding are responding to something else, like political or economic stability. The mean change in the sum total of funding at the country level across Latin America from one year to the next is a $18,209, all else being equal. Nevertheless, some states lose or gain hundreds of thousands of dollars in funding from year to year. The twenty-fifth percentile is a $100 increase and the seventy-fifth percentile is a $34,944 increase. Despite these fluctuations, regression results support the conclusion that the apparent correlation in Nicaragua is spurious. Year-to-year changes in funding are not more sensitive to political stability than is the general level of funding. The results are very similar to those in model 1 on table 6.1. For example, Ecuador had low political stability scores in 2011–12, but relatively strong funding, while Chile, Costa Rica, and Panama all had very high political stability scores in the late 2000s, but received very little funding. Once again, however, financial stability seems to be a major predictor of funding levels, as much for annual fluctuations within a country as for differences between countries.

These funding patterns might not be surprising to anybody who is familiar with the microfinance industry. The key ratings agencies mentioned above all focus their metrics and ratings primarily on financial sustainability. So, although poverty alleviation has long been part of the popular appeal of microfinance, and one of the main objectives of many, perhaps most, practitioners, investors have far less information about an MFI's impact on poverty alleviation than on its financial record. What information might be available tends to be somewhat vague. There are a number of studies that have purported to

**Table 6.1. Funding Decisions**

|  | (1)<br>Funding | (2)<br>Funding |
|---|---|---|
| Political stability | −4938.7 | |
|  | (1476.7) | |
| Financial stability | | 8612.2* |
|  | | (3827.7) |
| Number of borrowers | 0.0505*** | 0.0473*** |
|  | (0.00546) | (0.00483) |
| Microfinance regulatory environment | 5186.6** | 5070.7** |
|  | (1741.3) | (1557.4) |
| Population (millions) | −0.000291** | −0.000385** |
|  | (0.000108) | (0.000135) |
| % population below $2.50/day | 2486.3** | 3935.3*** |
|  | (801.9) | (441.3) |
| Constant | 58914.5 | −620565.8** |
|  | (145651.7) | (210767.2) |
| Observations | 41 | 41 |
| Wald $X^2$ | 17190.62 | 22767.89 |
| $R^2$ | 0.623 | 0.621 |

Panel Corrected Standard Errors in parentheses
* $p < 0.05$, ** $p < 0.01$, *** $p < 0.001$

show that microfinance affects poverty, but very few that show the conditions under which it is most effective, or even the conditions under which it might not have any beneficial impact on poverty. The best information that investors usually have to work from is that microfinance probably helps alleviate poverty, and that some institutions are better at reaching out to the very poor.[3] Beyond this, they have very little to guide them.

This is one of the reasons that people like Milford Bateman rail against microfinance; it is presented to us as an elegant solution to poverty alleviation, but the industry appears to be far more concerned with making profits, even off of the poorest and most vulnerable segments of society, than it is about poverty alleviation. Compartamos is an MFI that started in Mexico in 1990. It was financially successful for more than fifteen years. Then, in the mid-2000s, having grown to become one of the largest MFIs in the world, it made the move to become a publicly traded company. Compartamos made its IPO in April 2007, which generated massive profits for shareholders and executives throughout the institution. Some senior managers were rewarded with tens of millions of dollars (Bateman 2013). Mainstream investors, rather than social investors, bought most of the shares, representing 30% of bank ownership (Rosenberg 2007). While Compartamos had achieved the gold standard of financial viability, there were serious questions about its impact on poverty. The institution, which started out as an NGO and transitioned to a for-profit institution in 2000, was lending out huge quantities of money, but it was also charging rather high interest rates on the loans, in some cases approaching 200% annualized interest (Bateman 2010; Roodman 2012). Compare that to the 12–18% interest rates that sparked outrage and catalyzed the No Pago protests in Nicaragua. At this point we cannot help doubting that the poor are any better off as a result of this type of microfinance (Ghosh and Van Tassel 2013).

## IS MICROFINANCE THE RIGHT KIND OF HELP?

Microfinance is supposed to help the poor through two mechanisms. First, it provides them with lumps of capital they can use to purchase key inputs. Second, it provides them access to financial services, such as savings and future loans that will allow them to continue to make purchases into the future (Aghion and Morduch 2005). On the face of it, this makes sense. Neoliberal economic theory tells us that where capital is scarce, such as among the poor of a developing country, an influx of capital will greatly increase productive efficiency. In fact, the increase in productive efficiency should be large enough to outstrip returns on capital in economies that are capital intensive.

However, this does not bear out in the real world. In the real world investors tend to be very cautious about investing in developing countries. The majority of trade and of financial transactions occur between wealthy, developed countries, not between developed and developing countries (Chang 2014). This suggests that there is more at play than just the capital-to-labor ratio. Operating conditions for the MFI, or borrowing and spending conditions for the customers, matter.

While microfinance may indeed accomplish those objectives, it may not be the only, or even the best, mechanism for doing so. If the poor need access to capital to improve their financial situation, microfinance is attractive to development experts because once the first round of loans is repaid, the money can be used to continue to help more people. In an industry where there is never enough money, getting your money back every time seems like a great option. The problem is precisely that the poor have to give the money back every time. If what the poor need is capital, perhaps the better alternative would be to simply give them capital, no strings attached, no repayment necessary. This would, of course, require far more funding, but each recipient might feel a much larger impact on her financial situation. So, how does microfinance compare to cash transfer programs in terms of their ability to alleviate poverty?

Under President Fernando Cardoso, Brazil began a cash transfer program in the late 1990s that would eventually evolve into the Bolsa Família program.[4] The programs began with in-kind transfers such as cooking gas, or vouchers for in-kind transfers, such as food. The problem with in-kind transfers, however, is that it may or may not be what the family really needs. If food is what the family really needs then it is an efficient use of resources, but if the family is able to grow a large garden that would produce plenty of food except for the lack of fertilizer, then giving them food is a sub-optimal use of resources. The solution that the Brazilian government turned to was at the same time obvious and radical—give the recipients cash, rather than in-kind transfers. Obvious because giving people cash to spend on the things they need would be easier and a more efficient use of resources than in-kind transfers. It was also radical because many people believed that the poor were poor because they were not good at managing their resources. Giving them in-kind transfers takes much of the management out of their hands to prevent them from wasting their resources. Many people believed that cash transfers would induce the poor to spend all of the money at the bar, or put it to some other equally useless and perhaps damaging means.

Bolsa Família received a big boost to the program in 2003 when newly elected president "Lula" consolidated several pilot programs from around the country and made them universal across Brazil. He also increased funding for the program and established regulatory institutions that would track the program. It took some time to fully scale up, but today, the program is quite robust and reaches some eleven million households, or about forty million Brazilians (Houtzager 2008). The cash transfers are modest, and range up to R$200 (about US$65) per month for a family with three school-age children. The families that are eligible for the program are quite poor though, with average incomes around R$243 per month. Meanwhile, the program is relatively inexpensive, accounting for a mere 5% of the federal government's annual budget (Hall 2006).

Although CCTs are a relatively new approach to poverty alleviation, the effects of conditional cash transfer programs, as well as unconditional cash transfer programs, have been studied by many researchers. Most studies produce very positive results and development experts are generally quite optimistic about the programs' effectiveness for educational and health outcomes, among others. One of the conditions of most CCTs, including Bolsa Família, is that children must be consistently attending school. This has had a significant impact on enrollment and attendance, with some evidence that it is contributing to larger long-term impacts (Saavedra and Garcia 2013; Darney et al. 2013; Glewwe and Kassouf 2012). Another condition is that pregnant or lactating mothers and children must receive regular medical checkups and must meet minimum height-for-age requirements that often detect stunting caused by malnutrition. Again, the evidence is that this has helped improve health outcomes (Lagarde, Haines, and Palmer 2007; Fernald, Gertler, and Neufeld 2008; Rasella et al. 2013). So how do cash transfers compare to microfinance?

## Female Empowerment

One of the most attractive elements of microfinance to many activists is its ability to empower women. From the Grameen Bank in Bangladesh to CrediAmigo in Brazil, women make up the majority of microfinance customers, perhaps as much as 80% (Karlan and Goldberg 2011). This is by design (Mersland and Urgeghe 2013). The cultures of many developing countries are still male dominated. Men are typically seen as the primary income earners and are responsible for managing household finances. Women are tasked with cooking, cleaning and caring for children. It is often hoped that by providing loans to women, the women-recipients will have more influence over household finances and decision making (Cull, Demirgüç-Kunt, and Morduch 2009). Women are empowered because, often, only the woman of the house can access future loans from the MFI.

It is also often argued that women are more likely to spend more money on children's welfare than men do, by buying more and better food, clothes or education (Karlan and Goldberg 2011). Moreover, some studies have argued that women are more likely to repay their loans (Karlan and Zinman 2009). Moreover, by bringing women into the market, microfinance is mobilizing a largely untapped source of labor and pairing it with capital, which should have a significant impact on the household's finances, at least under the right conditions.[5]

Social investors and activists have picked up on this element of microfinance. Microfinance investors providing subsidized financing to MFIs are more likely to target MFIs that lend particularly, or exclusively, to women compared to MFIs that make no distinction between men and women (Mersland and Urgeghe 2013). Unsubsidized funding, on the other hand, does not seem to care whether an MFI targets men or women, on whether its finances are in order. Likewise, activists, such as those who make loans through Kiva.org, are more likely to target women (Jenq, Pan, and Theseira 2012; Ly and Mason 2012).

These same benefits are equally available through cash transfer programs. Bolsa Família, like many other CCTs, targets women in particular (Rawlings and Rubio 2005; Hall 2006). Among Latin American countries, as many as a third of poor households are headed by single women (Skidmore, Smith, and Green 2014). Excluding those poor households that are headed by single women, virtually all remaining households are jointly headed by a man and a woman. Bolsa Família cash disbursements are intended to be collected by mothers, rather than fathers, which should provide women with more influence over household finances and more equality with male family members.

Because of the health conditions required for the receipt of the cash transfer, the program ensures that children are receiving at least a basic level of nutrition and education, neither of which microfinance can guarantee. Bolsa Família might not go as far as some MFIs at putting women in control of household finances, but it also reaches more women. Where microfinance reaches a little over three million borrowers annually, only a portion of which are women and only a portion are from the poorest classes of society, Bolsa Família reaches approximately forty million of Brazil's poorest citizens and is easily accessible to all poor households. The person designated to receive the benefit is a woman in 93% of recipient households (Bruha 2014).

The Copenhagen Consensus Center has actually compared microfinance to CCTs directly. Their 2008 iteration of the Copenhagen Consensus examined "Women and Development" as one of their topics (King, Klasen, and Porter 2009). This means that the center commissioned papers looking at a handful of policy options or programs to advance women's position in terms of development. As part of the project the Copenhagen Consensus Center looks for a cost-benefit breakdown. They want to see what the expected return will be for each dollar spent on a particular proposal. CCT programs were the first proposal considered in their report. Based on available data, the report concluded that CCTs would provide returns of between $3 and $26.12 for every dollar spent, depending on the assumptions. These figures were based primarily on improving education for adolescent girls and paid little attention to the immediate and direct benefits provided through increased income and medical care. So, the real returns are likely considerably higher.

Microfinance was the second proposal the report considered. Like CCTs, the full effects of microfinance are difficult to calculate. The authors tried to make similar assumptions across analyses, though, again, the results likely underestimate the long-term effects of these programs. That said, the ratio ranges from $0.60 to $21.64. While both the lower bound and the upper bound, as well as median, are smaller for microfinance than for CCTs, the confidence intervals are wide enough that we cannot be terribly confident of the results. It is not entirely clear which type of program would be optimal. However, we can be far more confident that CCTs produce a positive net return, with a lower bound at $3 for every $1 spent, compared to microfinance with its lower bound at $0.60.

## Health Impacts

Health is one of the major concerns for the poor of any country. The poor, especially in rural areas, often have only limited access to basic preventative healthcare. Even in countries with nationalized healthcare systems, the poor often live farther away and have less means to travel to healthcare facilities (Sachs 2008). Globally, thousands of children die each day from easily cured diseases—those for which the scientific community has inexpensive cures that poor children simply do not have access to.[6] Aside from the costs of human suffering for the bereaved families of these children, it creates an economic drag far greater than people often realize. When a child is sick, somebody else in the family is often required to put off whatever else they might have been doing, such as a parent earning income or an older sibling attending school. The family is likely to pursue medical treatment, which may or may not be effective, but which will certainly cost a significant amount of money for the family. Then if the child dies, the family typically has to cover funeral costs of some sort. The situation is even worse if the family member who becomes ill is a key income earner. All of the same costs apply, but a major revenue stream dries up, so that the family is left with significant bills and no means of paying them, much less living at the same level as before. For many families living on the margin, a single illness can wipe out years of scrimping and saving (Krishna 2010).

Also, poor children are more likely to suffer from malnutrition, which can lead to physical stunting and impaired cognitive development (Rasella et al. 2013). Impaired development means that as these children mature into adulthood, they are less likely to have the same cognitive capacity that they might have achieved without suffering from malnutrition. In addition to stunting and malnutrition, hunger decreases children's ability to learn while in school. Consequently, they are more likely to drop out of school younger, to earn smaller incomes and to perpetuate the poverty cycle.

Microfinance has always been expected to help families cope with these problems. Microloans and micro-savings have both been shown to help smooth consumption (Duvendack et al. 2011). A family can take a loan to help them through a bad harvest, for example, without suffering severe hunger. It could also amortize the cost of life-saving medical treatment for a sick family member over several months, rather than having to pay all at once, or even upfront. It gives a household the financial flexibility they might need to in order to deal with unexpected costs. This should allow them to address health concerns more effectively. Intuitively, we expect people to address their basic needs if they can, beginning with food and water, shelter, and well-being. On the other hand, we might question how effectively a household can do this if the price of meeting immediate needs is a significant decline in future consumption as the household repays the loan plus interest.

The research on microfinance's impact on health outcomes is rather thin though. Some studies report modest increases in health outcomes (Montgomery and Weiss 2011). Other studies find no significant effect on health (Banerjee et al. 2013; Odell 2011). Still others say that microfinance might be used to improve health outcomes, but only under specific conditions (Duvendack et al. 2011). Microfinance may actually reduce health on one dimension, mental health, as people undergo additional stress while they try to repay their loans (Odell 2011). The evidence is not clear.

According to most research on cash transfers, however, giving poor people money has a consistent and significant impact on health outcomes. CCTs, such as Bolsa Família in Brazil, target health outcomes directly by requiring children and pregnant or lactating mothers to receive regular medical checkups. Studies have concluded that cash transfers are associated with improved height for age, suggesting that they are receiving better nutrition (Fernald, Gertler, and Neufeld 2008), presumably because children are eating more and better food, and because they are receiving regular medical checkups that can help fight off malnutrition through supplements. CCTs also consistently lower infant mortality across a variety of countries (Fiszbein and Schady

2009), and particularly lower the rate of deaths attributable to poverty-related problems such as malnutrition and diarrhea (Rasella et al. 2013). Mothers seem to be generally healthier as well and are less likely to die in childbirth (Fiszbein and Schady 2009). The effects are not stunningly large, but they are quite consistent across countries and over time.

## Cost and Funding

Program costs are an important element of any poverty alleviation effort. The amount of money that is available to devote to helping the poor is limited. So, the bang for the buck factor is critical. As has been mentioned a few times now, one of the real draws of microfinance for many investors and social activists is that their donation does not just help one family one time. It can go on helping over and over again. At least, that is the idea, though microfinance may or may not actually be helping the poor. The costs of the two programs are somewhat difficult to compare, since the funding structures are so different. Nonetheless, this is in itself a point of comparison.

The Brazilian federal government spent approximately R$21 billion (US$ 7 billion) on Bolsa Família in 2012, according to data from the Ministry for Social Development. Funding to the microfinance industry, on the other hand, fluctuates significantly. In 2011 it received just over US$ 500 million in funding. The total costs of these two programs are not even in the same ballpark, especially once we take into account that most, or all, of the microfinance funding will be repaid directly, while none of the CCT money will be. Moreover, most of the burden of paying for Bolsa Família is placed on Brazilian taxpayers, while the burden of paying for microfinance is put on the recipients themselves, paying out of their expected profits from the program.[7] So, while microfinance could hypothetically scale up indefinitely without putting any extra burden on the rest of the Brazilian population, the same is not true for the CCT program. For every additional Real that Brasília spends on Bolsa Família, it is one less Real that the government can spend on another program or that citizens can spend as they wish.

On the other hand, precisely because microfinance does not rely very heavily on the government for funding, it has been scaling up at a snail's pace. The reliance on philanthropic donations or complicated commercial funding means that many of the poor are left without access to capital. CCTs have upper limits on program size and budget, but reach more of the poor more quickly. They scale up by government decree. So, there are both pros and cons for the funding structures of both types of programs.

## Outreach

Outreach is one of the hotly debated aspects of microfinance. There are debates about who MFIs should be targeting. People have questioned whether microfinance can be genuinely considered social activism if MFIs fail to offer financial services to the poorest of the poor. Some MFIs, of course, are quite good at outreach, or making their services available to the poorest of the poor, to rural inhabitants, and to other marginalized groups of society, such as minorities and women. However, the MFIs that attract the most funding and that scale up the quickest are not usually those that perform well on measures of outreach (Cull, Demirgüç-Kunt, and Morduch 2009; Louis, Seret, and Baesens 2013). Many microfinance investors might be surprised to learn that the MFIs they are funding do not actually service the very poor.

The functional equivalent of this concept in the CCT literature is targeting. CCT programs target the poorest segment of the population and research shows that "CCT targeting is good" if not "perfect" (Zucco 2013). Being able to target the poorest of the poor means that CCT funds are going to the most vulnerable segment of society, rather than those who have enough experience and business acumen to turn a lump of capital into a productive enterprise or a more productive enterprise (Soares, Ribas, and Osório 2010). CCTs are equally available for the poor in major metropolises and for the poor in the most rural municipalities. Despite being a relatively new program, Bolsa Família reaches nearly four times as many households as microfinance does in Brazil.

## Microfinance Compared to Other Poverty Programs

In 2012, Bjørn Lomborg and the organization he helped create, the Copenhagen Consensus Center, put together a panel of five renowned economists, including four Nobel Laureates, to discuss the most cost-effective poverty interventions.[8] During the previous year, some fifty economists prepared their research in nearly forty different investment proposals for the expert panel to review. As part of the process the economists all traveled to Denmark to make the case for their proposal to the expert panel. This was the third iteration of this exercise, with previous conferences occurring in 2004 and 2008.[9]

After considering all of the proposals, the panel put them in rank order based on their cost-effectiveness for poverty alleviation, according to the best research the global social science community has to offer. In 2004, microfinance was still an up-and-coming intervention. As described previously, although it was growing quickly, it was still quite small. It was not included on the list of seventeen interventions. In 2008 the expert panel considered proposals on microfinance and included it on their list of interventions. It was ranked twenty-second for its ability to empower women, rather than for its ability to reduce malnutrition, improve education, decrease disease or affect any of the other issues the panel was considering.[10] The Copenhagen Consensus has never included microfinance on its lists of top interventions as a means of reducing disease, malnutrition, or any of the other problems the group considered. While microfinance was included in the list of interventions, other proposals were ranked as more efficient for advancing female empowerment. Other proposed interventions included increasing and improving girls' schooling through conditional cash transfers, ranked eighth, and providing support for women's reproductive role, ranked tenth.

In 2012, as in 2004, the panel did not include microfinance on the list, although this time the panel did not have a specific category for female empowerment. The challenges they considered included: armed conflict, biodiversity, chronic disease, climate change, education, hunger and malnutrition, infectious disease, natural disasters, population growth and water and sanitation (Lomborg 2014). Nonetheless, microfinance does not appear in the top thirty most cost-effective solutions to the challenges of poverty. CCTs, however, were ranked thirteenth, as the most cost-effective intervention for improving education. Although it is expected to increase incomes, which would allow families to buy more and better food, invest in education and access healthcare (Montgomery and Weiss 2011), many studies question these impacts and find no evidence that microfinance does any of these things (Banerjee et al. 2013). Even where research finds some impact, it is typically modest (Imai and Azam 2012).

So, when experts compare microfinance to alternative interventions designed to address malnutrition, educational outcomes and health issues, microfinance lags far behind in terms of cost-effectiveness. It falls even further behind when experts factor in future discounting to account for the lower value of an intervention that takes longer to produce the same results. Microfinance's absence from the list in 2012 is not surprising, considering the opposing results found in different studies and the lack of consistency. The results from previous chapters may resolve some of the inconsistencies of previous studies, but those same results also show that the impact of microfinance is modest at best.

Instead, the interventions that were at the top of the list in 2012 included programs that administer treatments for worms and diarrheal diseases, as well as provide micronutrients. These programs would address malnutrition in preschoolers and decrease hunger, so that children can focus on learning, as well as improve health so that children miss fewer days of school. The estimated return from de-worming children in Kenya was estimated to be twenty to fifty times higher than the cost (Lomborg 2014). Meanwhile, the microfinance literature is still debating whether microfinance even helps the poor, or whether it makes them worse off. It simply is not as effective as a poverty reduction mechanism.

## CONCLUSION

The evidence so far should raise some real concerns about microfinance as a poverty alleviation mechanism. Microfinance is not an effective poverty alleviation tool under many circumstances, and is potentially doing harm under some conditions. However, there are two major obstacles to tailoring its uses to situations where it is more likely to be effective. First, most people believe that it is universally useful for combating poverty. Second, funding structures will not be easy to change.

Within the academic community there are some microfinance skeptics like David Roodman and Milford Bateman. However, they are part of a small minority. Although several studies have been published in the last few years that add weight to the arguments against microfinance, there are also studies being published which argue that microfinance is beneficial, that it can reduce poverty. Many of these studies lack nuance in clarifying the conditions under which microfinance might be more or less effective, which fosters entrenchment by both sides because they can both find evidence that supports their case. The skeptics find evidence in randomized controlled trials and a handful of quantitative studies, while the believers rely on case studies and different quantitative studies (Cull, Demirgüç-Kunt, and Morduch 2009). Adding nuance to the discussion may help bring these two sides closer together.

On the other hand, changes in the academic literature will not necessarily bring about changes in the microfinance industry. Practitioners, generally speaking, still seem to be quite confident about microfinance as a poverty alleviation mechanism. NGOs like CGAP and ACCION continue to support microfinance in a variety of ways, from offering funding and technical expertise to commissioning research on best practices or tracking metrics that help MFIs in their day-to-day operations. IGOs are in the same boat. The World Bank continues to support microfinance as a poverty alleviation mechanism too. Its website describes microfinance as helping families build assets, manage risks and smooth consumption (*Microfinance and Financial Inclusion: At a Glance* 2014). It suggests that microfinance allows children to spend more time in school because their families are in better financial positions. However, there is some evidence that as a family's microenterprise starts to pick up business, thanks to its microloan, children, particularly older children, are often pulled into the family business before finishing schooling (Augsburg et al. 2012). But the World Bank is not alone; other global IGOs such as the Organization for Economic Cooperation and Development (OECD) and regional IGOs like the Inter-American Development Bank (IADB) also continue to support microfinance operations through funding and publishing information on best practices. They also support microfinance by publishing information about how closely MFIs follow best practices, which other major financiers use to make decisions about investing in microfinance.

While the academic literature is beginning to seriously question microfinance as a poverty alleviation mechanism, this healthy skepticism does not appear to be carrying over to practitioners. This means that the funding structures will likely remain unchanged for quite some time. This is in part due to the way people, including investors, practitioners and individuals, think about microfinance. For nearly a decade, a significant part of the microfinance discussion has been about the role of for-profit MFIs. The discussion is symptomatic of the rise of profit-oriented MFIs. On the one hand, profit-oriented ventures can scale up much faster than non-profits because they can offer something that makes business sense for investors. In the case of institutions like Compartamos in Mexico, it makes a lot of business sense for investors; millions of dollars' worth of business sense, in fact. Investors look at the data being collected and published by theMIX.org and see that some MFIs are safer bets than others and some offer better returns on investment than others. Investors are certainly attracted by the extremely high repayment rates that most MFIs boast. In many cases, repayment rates are actually higher than in some commercial loan sectors. So it turns out that many investors are not thinking about microfinance as a poverty alleviation mechanism, but rather they are thinking about how microfinance contributes to their profit margin.

Likewise, at the individual level, since most people believe that microfinance is universally beneficial to microfinance customers, they feel good about contributing to and supporting the microfinance industry (Moss, Neubaum, and Meyskens 2014). Kiva, for example, was started by social entrepreneurs, people who wanted to make a positive difference in the world. Lenders make no profit on the money they lend. They lend the money because they believe they are contributing to global poverty alleviation. Indeed, they are told, in no uncertain terms, by Kiva, the World Bank, OECD, IADB, and many other supposed experts, that microfinance is beneficial. They have no reason to doubt its positive impact.

Until people start to pick up on the skepticism that is growing in the academic literature, they are not likely to change their modus operandi. Investors will continue to see microfinance as a profitable venture and treat it as such. NGOs and IGOs will continue to speak of microfinance as a terrific poverty alleviation mechanism and convince socially minded individuals that they should continue to support the global microfinance industry if they want to help the poor. Neither extreme is correct though. The answer lies somewhere in the middle. Microfinance can have a positive impact on the poor, but only under the right conditions. Microfinance is not useless, but neither is it a cure-all. Using microfinance effectively requires thoughtfulness and careful analysis to determine where it might be useful and where it might not. Unfortunately, that message is not one that appears likely to catch on anytime soon, and will only garner support with time if practitioners and activists begin to take notice.

## NOTES

1. Bolivia represents the high end of deposit mobilization to fund MFIs where it accounts for as much as 60% of funding. On the other hand, in countries like Brazil, government regulations prevent deposit mobilization by anything other than a fully regulated, commercial financial institution, or in other words, a bank (Kumar 2005).

2. Some of the agencies that rate MFIs include MicroRate.com, PlanetRating. com, MicroFinanzaRating.com, as well as MIXMarket.org. The various agencies use slightly different methodologies to rate MFIs, but they all look at things like basic finance, how much money the institution is lending out, how much interest it is charging, what the overhead costs are, and so on. Much of this information is self-reported to the ratings agencies and then spot-checked by the agency. The MFIs who report are generally happy to do so because it puts them in a better position to secure additional funding. It also means, however, that the ratings agencies over-represent the most established and largest MFIs and under-represent smaller, newer and less-efficient MFIs.

3. Ironically, the MFIs that are most likely to reach out to the very poor are also least likely to receive a lot of funding because they tend to be financially weaker (Wiesner and Quien 2010; Mersland and Urgeghe 2013).

4. Mexico also began a conditional cash transfer program about the same time as Brazil, and which followed a very similar trajectory in its evolution. The present Mexican program is called Oportunidades. Its objectives and outcomes have been very similar to those in Brazil. These two programs spurred the creation of conditional cash transfer programs around the world. There are today conditional cash transfer programs on five continents.

5. As noted previously, the dramatic impact on the economy has not panned out. However, this does not necessarily mean that the other potential effects of lending to women do not exist.

6. The hundreds of thousands figure is down considerably from just a couple of decades ago when the figure was well into the millions. The fourth Millennium Development Goal was to reduce under-five mortality by two-thirds. Globally, we have missed the goal, although some regions, including Latin America, have achieved it.

7. I say here that most of the cost of Bolsa Família is paid for by Brazilian taxpayers because it is a government program that is largely funded through taxes. However,

the Brazilian government has also received some notable grants from the World Bank to develop and improve the program.

8. Panel members included Robert Mundell, 1999 winner of the Nobel Prize in Economics; Vernon Smith, co-recipient, along with Daniel Kahneman, of the 2002 Nobel Memorial Prize in Economic Sciences; Nancy Stokey, the Frederick Henry Prince Distinguished Service Professor of Economics at the University of Chicago; Thomas Schelling, co-recipient with Robert Aumann of the 2005 Nobel Memorial Prize in Economic Sciences; and Finn Kydland, co-recipient with Edward Prescott of the 2004 Nobel Memorial Prize in Economic Sciences.

9. The panel members change from one iteration to the next. There is some consistency though. Thomas Schelling, Vernon Smith and Nancy Stokey have participated in all three rounds.

10. The 2008 panel concerned itself with malnutrition, trade, diseases, education, female empowerment, global warming, access to clean drinking water, air pollution and terrorism.

# Chapter Seven

# The Future of Microfinance

The first chapter of this book presented microfinance as a poverty alleviation mechanism that is qualitatively different from other mechanisms typically discussed by the development community. Microfinance is different because the government is not directly involved in the distribution of microfinance, and often plays only a small role in funding it. It also puts money directly into the hands of the poor. It relies on the market for much of its funding and allows poor households to use the market to improve their quality of life. However, the differences between microfinance and other types of interventions may not be as significant as some have suggested.

Foreign aid, for example, might function as a poverty alleviation mechanism when it is used to build infrastructure, fund education or provide critical resources like food and water. Aid is generally given from one government to another. Its effectiveness as a poverty alleviation mechanism depends on the recipient's ability and desire to use it for productive purposes, but all too often it is used to line the pockets of the leadership while those who sincerely need help see little or no benefit from it (Hubbard and Duggan 2009). Aid also comes with strings attached in most cases. For example, the donor state might require the recipient to spend the money on goods and services originating from the donor state, which limits the recipient's ability to use the aid effectively (Easterly 2006). Moreover, because the donor states usually put a low priority on aid relative to domestic concerns, aid can be inconsistent during times of economic stress and this inconsistency can dramatically reduce its effectiveness for poverty alleviation (Kodama 2012). Finally, there is evidence that political instability reduces the effectiveness of aid for poverty alleviation (Chauvet and Guillamont 2003).

None of this should be surprising since aid is also often seen by donor states as a cheap way of influencing the recipient state. If a donor state can buy the recipient state's attention for $20 million, the donor's policy gains might well more than compensate for the money given in aid. Hans Morgenthau argued that all foreign aid is political, with the occasional exception of disaster relief aid (Morgenthau 1962). He also explained that foreign aid should be accepted as part of foreign policy; it fills a gap that military action and traditional diplomacy cannot. It is an example of coercion via carrots rather than sticks. Accepting Morgenthau's premise, aid that is given for political purposes likely does not have development as its objective since successful development would weaken the donor state's influence as the recipient's economy grew.

Foreign investment, whether direct or portfolio investment, has been promoted as another effective mechanism for poverty alleviation since it can create jobs in factories or mineral extraction companies while also spurring the economy forward through capital accumulation and knowledge dispersion in productive sectors of the economy. Investment, like aid, is also closely connected to the state. It tends to be carefully regulated by the state and can be subject to taxes and restrictions. Its effectiveness for poverty alleviation and durability are dependent on profit incentives, which are sensitive to currency fluctuations, monetary policy, fiscal policy and political and economic stability (Busse and Hefeker 2007; Daude and Stein 2007). Portfolio investment tends to be flighty, departing at the first hint of trouble, often at the moment when the state most needs a stable economy. Because of its flightiness, foreign investment has been dubbed the "electronic herd" by Thomas Friedman, alluding to its tendency to stampede without warning, often undermining long-term development by destroying whatever might get in the way of profits (Friedman 2005). Debt forgiveness programs, structural adjustment loans and joint development projects are all subject to the same whims of the donor state as aid and investment (Balaam and Dillman 2011; Easterly 2006). Direct investment is more stable than portfolio investment in the short term, but is also highly sensitive to the macro conditions present in the country. Investors are generally even more responsive to the rule of law and effective functioning of courts, as well as political and economic stability.

Microfinance is different. Governments can regulate microfinance, but they do not generally disburse it. Governments sometimes fund microfinance, but they do not usually benefit directly from it. Where aid usually operates at the state level, and investment operates at the societal level, microfinance operates at the individual or household level. Once an MFI is properly funded and operating, it often does not require continued support from a donor or investor. Perhaps most importantly, the funds are given directly to the poor and decisions about how to use the money are made by the recipients, the poor households who desperately need financial help. If we assume that the poor are able to make strategic financial decisions as well as anybody else, this means they may become uniquely suited to addressing their most binding constraints when financial resources are made available.

Since microfinance has a qualitatively different relationship to the state than do foreign aid and most forms of foreign investment, many so-called experts in microfinance have assumed that the relationship is negligible. This assumption does not seem, at first glance, to be too unreasonable, and perhaps for some aspects of microfinance it is not. However, there are some reasons to believe that microfinance may not be all that different from other poverty alleviation approaches in terms of how variations in the quality of governance might modify the impact on poverty. The puzzle that motivated this research project is the discrepancy between findings of various microfinance impact analyses. Many studies have found that microfinance is always, or nearly always, positive (Brau, Hiatt, and Woodworth 2004; Brau and Woller 2004; Imai, Arun and Annim 2010; Schicks 2007). Based on the academic literature and reports and projects coming out of international organizations like the development-focused NGO ACCION, or the Inter-American Development Bank, most practitioners seem to believe that microfinance, at worst, has no effect, and at best can dramatically change poor people's lives for the better by providing them with a stepping stone from which they can eventually make their way out of poverty and onto solid financial ground. On the other hand, a number of other scholars have found evidence that microfinance is at best ineffective and at worst very damaging (Karlan and Zinman 2009; Roodman 2012).

These opposing positions, both from some carefully planned and executed research designs, suggest a couple of possible conclusions. Some scholars have suggested that there are cultural factors that have not yet been accounted for (Epstein and Yuthas 2010), that microfinance is not always being properly managed and implemented (Field and Pande 2007; Hermes and Lensink 2007), or that it has to do with the demographics of the people whom an MFI serves (Remenyi and Quinones 2000), among others. The argument posed at the beginning of this book is that one of the factors that matters is governance—political institutions and political and economic stability. The argument is based on the notion that greater certainty about the future makes investment decisions easier and more efficient, and that instability will complicate those decisions. It has long been accepted that uncertainty in the state or the economy makes investment riskier and, therefore, generally less efficient since investors would be risking too much to safely maximize leverage on their assets (Pindyck 1993). Three hypotheses were developed and tested.

H1: *Regardless of the microfinance industry, governments with quality insti-*
*tutions will have lower poverty levels than governments with poor institu-*
*tions.*

H2: *Regardless of the quality of government institutions, greater microfi-*
*nance outreach will lead to lower poverty levels.*

H3: *The higher the quality of governmental institutions, the greater the pov-*
*erty reduction effect of microfinance.*

The results reaffirmed that better governance generally leads to lower poverty levels and vice versa. This was not an original or unexpected finding, but it helped set the stage for subsequent hypotheses. Hypothesis two was rejected in testing for hypothesis three. Regression results showed that not only do governmental institutions modify the poverty alleviation effect of microfinance, but under the wrong conditions, microfinance actually leaves the poor worse off. Therefore, greater microfinance outreach will not always lead to lower levels of poverty. Only under the right conditions will that happen.

Chapter 4 used regression analysis to examine the interaction between the number of microfinance borrowers in a state for a given year, and different measures of institutional quality and stability to predict infant mortality, the proxy for poverty. Only some of the institutions tested in the analysis significantly modified the impact microfinance has on poverty. The level of coverage by either public or private credit monitoring agencies had no statistically significant impact. Law and order did though. In fact, where law and order were weakest, analyses showed that microfinance actually exacerbates poverty rather than alleviating it, but above a certain minimum threshold, a marginal increase in the level of law and order did not increase microfinance effectiveness. Political and economic stability both affected microfinance too. For each one, where stability was lowest, microfinance was predicted to increase poverty rather than decrease it, the same as law and order. However, unlike law and order, the model predicted that marginal increases of both political and economic stability would strengthen the poverty alleviation effect of microfinance. Once again, though, for both political and economic stability, a state only had to achieve modest levels of stability before the negative impact turned positive.

The substantive effects, though statistically significant, were modest. Based on regression results reported in table 4.4 and figures 4.1 and 4.2, in the most economically stable states, microfinance might reduce infant mortality by as much as 3.5 deaths per 10,000 live births. That represents roughly an additional 35% reduction in infant mortality beyond what we would expect without microfinance, just from normal economic growth and rising incomes, greater access to healthcare, and better health technology. On the other hand, in states where law and order is weak, microfinance may drive up infant mortality by as much as 4 per 10,000 live births. This could actually reverse the progress being made in reducing infant mortality for those countries—a disastrous outcome.

Chapter 5 presented a case study of microfinance in Brazil. The chapter discussed the political and economic turmoil that plagued Brazil from the 1930s to the present. It then examined how the microfinance industry developed and evolved in Brazil. Once microfinance gained a significant presence, around the late 1990s, those states within Brazil which had more microfinance saw poverty reduction far superior to those in the rest of the country during a five-year period in which Brazil's economy and political sphere were only moderately stable. Interestingly, though, and in keeping with findings from chapter 4, it appears that better governance improves the poverty alleviation impact of microfinance. This time, however, it is better governance at the local level. Santa Catarina, a state in the southern region of the country, which consistently outshines the Northeast in quality of governance indicators, and which had a uniquely advanced microfinance industry for the region, saw more poverty alleviation than any other state. After 2003, the federal government launched a handful of other poverty alleviation programs, which nearly washed out the effect of microfinance.

The evidence clearly shows that microfinance can work, at least under the right conditions. But at what cost? Under the wrong conditions, microfinance appears to be harmful. In fact, the negative impact of microfinance operating under poor conditions may be greater than the positive impact it has when operating under the best conditions. To make matters worse, microfinance is no longer simply funded by philanthropic donations and a few government grants. Microfinance Investment Vehicles (MIVs) mobilize money from international banks and major investors worldwide and channel it to MFIs in the developing world. Global MIV assets sum to more than eight billion dollars. Unfortunately, the evidence shows that the big money behind the global microfinance industry does not seem to care all that much about poverty alleviation, only about return on investment. On the other end of the spectrum, even small, socially motivated microfinance lenders seem to be unaware that microfinance may be harming the very people they are trying to help. Moreover, the positive impact microfinance has on poverty is modest. Even where microfinance operates under ideal conditions, other poverty alleviation programs may be more cost-effective. Chapter 6 dealt with these issues and suggested that policy makers and practitioners should be cautious about microfinance.

## THEORETICAL IMPLICATIONS

The results of this study have three major theoretical implications. First, risk and uncertainty appear to have similar impacts on microfinance effectiveness as on other development-related sectors. Second, studies like David Rood-man's (2012) found that microfinance is not helpful, and studies like Imai, Arun and Annim's (2010) found that microfinance generally reduces poverty at the household level; both are only partially correct. Third, the conclusions support Popkin's rational peasant argument that the poor make investments, even under risk, in order to improve their economic situation.

Since foreign aid and FDI are both sensitive to risk and instability, it makes sense that microfinance should be too (Busse and Hefeker 2007; Chauvet and Guillamont 2004; Hubbard and Duggan 2009; Kolstad and Villanger 2008). Risk does indeed affect microfinance. Instability hinders the poor and microenterprises the same way it hinders larger firms and wealthier households. Weak law and order means that people, whether poor or wealthy, can be less confident that their property will remain undamaged and in their possession. This would reduce their incentive to invest in future profits and would likely force them to invest less efficiently as they try to hedge against potential loss.

Political instability might come in a variety of forms, from peaceful protests that impede commerce, to riots or even war, which destroy capital. The risk of this type of an event might deter the poor from using capital as effectively as they might otherwise. Perhaps the very poor are reticent to take risks because they recognize that they are only one financial shock away from total ruin (Krishna 2010). If the very poor take a loan and the intended productive use does not pan out, the individual is left with an additional demand on her resources as she tries to repay the loan, but no additional income with which to do so. Political instability hinders most sectors of the economy through a variety of mechanisms, such as changing policies and regulations, corruption, bureaucratic ineffectiveness or social unrest. Where these are more common, or more likely to occur, the poor are less likely to benefit from the financial services offered by the microfinance sector.

Economic stability has the same effects, though the mechanisms differ somewhat. Rather than protests, corruption and war, it is changing currency values, weak economic growth and price fluctuations that hinder microfinance effectiveness. The poor are at least as sensitive to the consumer price index as large enterprises because the poor live constantly on the margin. If they have a bad quarter, it doesn't just drive down stock prices, it may mean that the family misses meals or cannot access needed medical services. The stakes are high for the poor.

The effect of instability is useful information for the continued development of microfinance because it suggests that a risk hedging approach might be more effective than an asset accumulation approach to microfinance services (Islam 2009). That is, microfinance institutions might have a greater effect on poverty in less stable countries by offering insurance services that would reduce risk for the very poor, so that if an income earner is put out of work or the economy slows, the household still has the means to meet their basic needs. This does not directly provide a poor household with assets that can be invested to increase income, but it might allow the household to reallocate assets by reinvesting them in productive capital and pulling them away from rainy-day savings, which are often zero interest and held in the home or with a friend or family member (Collins et al. 2009).

The second major theoretical contribution of this work is to present a key consideration that might modify the results of many past studies. Some scholars have found evidence that microfinance is useful for poverty alleviation and others have found that it is not. They might both be partially correct. The research here shows that microfinance can be both effective and ineffective at poverty alleviation. Variations can occur from one country to the next and they can occur within the same country at different points in time depending on whether there are significant changes in government institutions and stability. This is a major step forward for microfinance research. It helps move the debate from whether microfinance works to when and where it works, and how to use it most effectively as a poverty alleviation mechanism.

Finally, Samuel Popkin argued that peasants are rational (1979). More specifically, he showed that peasants do not have romantic perceptions of their positions as laborers, but rather they are primarily interested in securing their long-term economic well-being. Peasants, though poor, are often willing to invest what little they might be able to scrape together if they believe it will improve their future economic position. The results from chapters 4 and 5 support Popkin's argument. They show that, under the right conditions, the poor are able to effectively invest and take risks, in order to improve their economic standing. In fact, based on loan repayment rates, microfinance borrowers, that is the poor, do this at least as well as, and perhaps better than, average debtors. This conclusion counters the long-standing assumption implicit in many social welfare programs that if you give cash to poor people, they will waste it.

## IMPLICATIONS FOR PRACTITIONERS

Microfinance practitioners are aware that microfinance has the ability to improve the quality of life of their customers. There is plenty of anecdotal evidence that people's lives improve when they have access to financial services (Roodman 2012). Simple logic suggests that this should be the case if one assumes that potential customers are wise enough to know when they can improve their position through financial services and when they cannot. If a poor person needs access to financial services and an MFI is operating in her village, and that MFI offers the type of services the individual needs, then she can utilize those services to her benefit, at least if the price is right. If there is an MFI in a person's village, but that person cannot improve her quality of life by patronizing its services, then she will, presumably, not do so and no harm is done. On the other hand, if there is no MFI, or the MFI does not offer the types of services the person needs, then she does not have the opportunity to improve her quality of life. Therefore, a good deal of the conversation about microfinance effectiveness among practitioners revolves around the types of services MFIs offer and their target audiences. When practitioners acknowledge the role of the state, it is generally to discuss regulations that affect the MFIs' ability to innovate and offer the kinds of services the poor need, rather than the risk it may present.

Practitioners need to realize that there is more to it than that though. The quality of governance does not only affect MFIs. It affects the poor as well, and specifically their ability to use microfinance in a way that improves their quality of life. The development community became very excited about microfinance around the turn of the century because of its unique relationship with the state and its direct interaction with the poor. It seemed like a good solution to a problem that the market could not address. In some ways, this is true. Microfinance meets a demand that the market often fails to provide for. However, the costs of doing so are not uniform across cases. Microfinance might be a good option for promoting poverty alleviation in some countries, but practitioners should not expect that what works well in Chile will work just as well in El Salvador. The macro conditions are too different. The political and economic stability in Chile means that microfinance customers are better able to allocate their resources efficiently, but their counterparts in El Salvador will have less ability to do so. Perhaps the Salvadoran holds back some of her resources to protect her assets from theft or vandalism, or perhaps she must hedge against corruption or societal violence. Likewise, the Salvadoran micro-borrower is more likely to encounter circumstances that will limit her ability to continue making a profit. If that is the case, she is left with an additional debt obligation to service, but no additional income. She is, therefore, made worse off as a result of microfinance.

Microfinance can be beneficial, but it can be harmful too. A practitioner who is devoted to the social cause often associated with microfinance must be discerning in where and how microfinance is applied as a mechanism for poverty alleviation. It should not be thought of as useful in combating poverty in countries where the rule of law is weak, or where the political or economic environments are unstable. Unfortunately, this means that many of the poorest countries are not likely to benefit from microfinance since the poorest also typically have the weakest state capacity to enforce laws and create and maintain effective institutions and policies.

In Latin America, this means that Nicaragua, which has a GDP per capita of less than US$2,000, making it one of the poorest countries in the region, is not a good candidate for microfinance. Nicaragua consistently suffers from poor economic stability. Despite its moderate performance on political stability and the rule of law, the negative effects of economic instability will, on average, overwhelm any benefits microfinance could offer and have a net negative impact on poverty in the country. Likewise, Honduras, which is only slightly wealthier, on average, than Nicaragua, is moderately stable in the political sphere and generally stable in the economic sphere as well. However, Honduras consistently struggles with law and order. It is prone to violence and lawlessness related to drug trafficking, for example; a problem that plagues virtually all of Central America. In addition to the drug cartels, or in part because of them, personal violence in Honduras is astronomical. It has one of the highest homicide rates in the world (Weeks 2015). Because of the government's inability to curb violence and protect individual security, Hondurans also report some of the lowest levels in the world of confidence in the government.

These are the people who need help the most. They live in poverty, personal violence is rampant, and they have very little hope that their own government can or will do anything to improve the situation. Unfortunately, microfinance is not likely to benefit Hondurans or Nicaraguans. The difficulty is that foreign aid is not likely to do much good either and neither foreign nor domestic entities are excited about investing in these countries in any way that is going to raise incomes or improve governance.

The good news is that there are a number of countries that might be able to benefit from microfinance. Peru and Bolivia both have the right conditions for effective microfinance and both have rather large domestic microfinance industries. However, Chile, which is the Latin American country best suited for microfinance effectiveness, at least in terms of the quality of governance, has one of the lowest levels of microfinance penetration in the region. This could be because it is also one of the wealthiest states in the region, with GDP per capita over US$15,000. However, Panama and Costa Rica, which are not nearly as well off as Chile, both display good conditions for microfinance, but also have very limited microfinance industries. On the other hand, Nicaragua, despite having conditions that are likely to make microfinance counter-productive, has one of the strongest microfinance industries in the region, comparable even to Peru and Bolivia. The lack of correlation between the conditions that allow microfinance to combat poverty and where funding for microfinance goes does not suggest that microfinance investors are particularly concerned about poverty alleviation. Microfinance could be far more effective if practitioners would implement microfinance more cautiously.

There are lessons here for policy makers too. Policy makers in Nicaragua should be weary of the microfinance industry in their country. Regulations that protect the poor would likely help stanch the negative effects it is otherwise likely to have. Although many people decried Brazil's anti-usury laws and regulations that prohibited non-financial institutions from doing some of the things that banks could do (Olsen 2010; Demirgüç-Kunt and Morduch 2011), there may be wisdom behind those laws since Brazil often performs poorly on law and order. Based on the results of this study, policy makers should use this information to focus on improving governance and institutions to the point that microfinance is likely to have a positive impact rather than a negative impact.

While states that do not have the right conditions for microfinance effectiveness should be wary of microfinance, states that do have the right conditions might still not necessarily want to embrace it wholeheartedly. Microfinance can have a positive impact on poverty, but its effect is still limited. Previous research has shown that the poorest of the poor are generally still left without access to financial services as the microfinance industry caters to the not-so-poor (Thapa 2010; Duvendack et al. 2011). This suggests that microfinance could only be a piece of the development model for a state.

Another problem is that the effects of microfinance, even under the best conditions, are somewhat modest. Significant increases in microfinance often yield rather modest changes in poverty measures. The treatment effect used throughout the book was an increase of fifty borrowers per thousand population, which might reduce infant mortality by three or four per 10,000 live births. However, that kind of growth in the microfinance industry requires years to achieve. Most states will take eight to ten years of steady growth to achieve that kind of increase in microfinance. The return is not all that impressive for such a large investment. So, policy makers should consider other poverty alleviation programs that might be more cost-effective. One thing we have learned from the research that might help policy makers to implement more cost-effective programs is that, given the right conditions, the poor appear to be quite capable of using resources effectively to improve their quality of life (Collins et al. 2009).

All of this should be considered valuable information to individual MFIs, as well as the sundry international organizations that concern themselves with poverty and development. The beginning of this project mentioned the UN's Millennium Development Goals. Understanding how poverty alleviation mechanisms work is critical for achieving those goals. Allowing microfinance to continue on as it has up to this point is not making enough progress towards those objectives. Thus, significant resources intended to combat poverty are tied up in programs that potentially aggravate it. As a global community, we cannot eliminate global poverty without better policies, which requires a better, more complete understanding of the tools being used to fight it.

As the technologies and networks that are being forged by globalization continue to advance, the global community must continue to concern itself with poverty alleviation. Many people heralded microfinance as the way forward; a way to draw the poor into the global financial network. Global banking thought it had hit a home run with the double-bottom line of microfinance: poverty alleviation and profits. However, empirical analysis shows that global financial resources are not being efficiently allocated (see chapter 6). Too much microfinance funding is going to countries where it is more likely to harm the poor than to help them. Moreover, it is not clear that microfinance is even a very effective or efficient way to help the poor, when compared to other types of interventions. Global banking, instead of hitting a home run on the double-bottom line of microfinance has only hit a single, making profits without having much impact on poverty. Worst of all, it is the poor who most often strike out when their governments fail to foster the kinds of institutions that benefit the poor along with the economy at large.

This book has carefully examined microfinance effectiveness and found that it is not the panacea many people believe it to be. All too often, it is counter-productive, ensnaring the poor in debt traps that will reduce their already meager incomes. Microfinance can contribute to easing poverty, but only under the right conditions—conditions that are unlikely to be found among the poorest countries. Therefore, despite the good intentions of socially conscious individuals who invest or donate money to the microfinance industry through Kiva.org and other avenues, those funds are unlikely to be doing much good. The World Bank maintains that microfinance should continue to expand in order to provide financial services to everybody in the world. However, the evidence contrasts sharply with this assertion. Instead, microfinance should shrink, at least geographically, to concentrate on alleviating poverty in countries with stable political and economic environments and strong law and order. Outside of those countries, microfinance is exacerbating poverty. The global development community needs to move past this infatuation with microfinance and continue searching for interventions that actually alleviate poverty on a large scale.

# Bibliography

Acemoglu, Daron, and James Robinson. 2012. *Why Nations Fail: The Origins of Power, Prosperity, and Poverty.* New York: Crown Business.

Adler, Emanuel, and Peter Haas. 1992. "Conclusion: Epistemic Communities, World Order, and the Creation of a Reflective Research Program." *International Organization* 46 (1): 367–90.

Aghion, Beatrice, and Jonathan Morduch. 2005. *The Economics of Microfinance.* Cambridge: MIT Press.

Agresti, Alan, and Barbara Finlay. 1997. *Statistical Methods for the Social Sciences.* 3rd ed. Upper Saddle River, NJ: Prentice-Hall.

Ahlin, C., N. Jiang, and D. Paper. 2005. "Can Micro-Credit Bring Development?" *Working* D82, O11.

Ahlin, Christian, Jocelyn Lin, and Michael Maio. 2011. "Where Does Microfinance Flourish? Microfinance Institution Performance in Macroeconomic Context." *Journal of Development Economics* 95 (2): 105–20. doi:10.1016/j.jdeveco.2010.04.004.

Alesina, Alberto, and David Dollar. 2000. "Who Gives Foreign Aid to Whom and Why?" *Journal of Economic Growth* 5 (1): 33–63. doi:10.1023/a:1009874203400.

Alves, Maria Helena Moreira. 1985. *State and Opposition in Military Brazil.* Austin: University of Texas Press.

Amann, Edmund. 2003. "Economic Policy and Performance in Brazil since 1985." In *Brazil since 1985: Politics, Economy and Society,* edited by Maria D'Alva Kinzo and James Dunkerly. London: Institute of Latin American Studies, University of London.

Andrade, Pablo, and Liisa North. 2011. "Ecuador: Political Turmoil, Social Mobilization, and a Turn Toward the Left." In *Latin America: Its Problems and Its Promise,* edited by Jan Knippers Black, 5th ed., 413–28. Boulder, CO: Westview Press.

Anirudh, Krishna. 2010. *One Illness Away: Why People Become Poor and How They Escape Poverty.* New York: Oxford University Press.

Annim, Samuel Kobina. 2012. "Targeting the Poor Versus Financial Sustainability and External Funding: Evidence of Microfinance Institutions in Ghana." *Journal of Developmental Entrepreneurship* 17 (03): 1250016. doi:10.1142/S1084946712500161.

Aubert, Cecile, Alain de Janvry, and Elisabeth Sadoulet. 2009. "Designing Credit Agent Incentives to Prevent Mission Drift in Pro-Poor Microfinance Institutions." *Journal of Development Economics* 90 (1): 153–62.

Augsburg, Britta, Ralph De Haas, Heike Harmgart, and Costas Meghir. 2012. *Microfinance at the Margin: Experimental Evidence from Bosnia and Herzegovina*. W12/15. London. http://dx.doi.org/10.1920/wp.ifs.2012.1215.

Ault, Joshua K., and Andrew Spicer. 2009. "Does One Size Fit All in Microfinance?: New Directions for Academic Research." In *Moving Beyond Storytelling: Emerging Research in Mircrofinance*, edited by T. Wuerth and A. Watkins. Amsterdam: Elsevier.

Aytac, S. E. 2013. "Distributive Politics in a Multiparty System: The Conditional Cash Transfer Program in Turkey." *Comparative Political Studies* 47 (9): 1211–37. doi:10.1177/0010414013495357.

Baer, Werner. 2001. *The Brazilian Economy: Growth and Development*. 5th ed. Westport, CT: Praeger.

Baird, Sarah, Ephraim Chirwa, Craig Mcintosh, and Berk Ozler. 2010. "The Short-Term Impacts of a Schooling Conditional Cash Transfer Program on the Sexual Behavior of Young Women." *Health Economics* 19: 55–68. doi:10.1002/hec.

Baker, Andy. 2014. *Shaping the Developing World: The West, the South, and the Natural World*. Thousand Oaks, CA: Sage.

Balaam, David, and Bradford Dillman. 2009. *Introduction to International Political Economy*. 5th ed. Boston: Longman.

Banerjee, Abhijit, Esther Duflo, Rachel Glennerster, and Cynthia Kinnan. 2013. *The Miracle of Microfinance? Evidence from a Randomized Evaluation*. MIT Department of Economics Working Paper. 13–09.

Barro, Robert. 1997. *Determinants of Economic Growth: A Cross-Country Empirical Study*. Cambridge, MA: MIT Press.

Barry, Thierno Amadou, and Ruth Tacneng. 2014. "The Impact of Governance and Institutional Quality on MFI Outreach and Financial Performance in Sub-Saharan Africa." *World Development* 58 (June). Elsevier Ltd: 1–20. doi:10.1016/j.worlddev.2013.12.006.

Bateman, Milford. 2010. *Why Microfinance Doesn't Work? The Destructive Rise of Local Neoliberalism*. London: Zed Books.

———. 2013. *The Age of Microfinance: Destroying Latin American Economies from the Bottom Up*. 39. Ola Financiera. http://networkideas.org/networkideas/pdfs/age_microfinance.pdf.

BBC News. 2010. "Ecuador Declares State of Emergency Amid 'Coup Attempt,'" October 1.

———. 2014. "Hong Kong Protests May Cost Retailers HK$2bn Says ANZ Bank," October 3. http://www.bbc.com/news/business-29470815.

Beck, Nathaniel, and Jonathan N. Katz. 1995. "What to Do (and Not to Do) with Time-Series Cross-Section Data." *American Political Science Review* 89 (3): 634–47.

Beck, Thorsten, Asli Demirgüç-Kunt, and Ross Levine. 2007. "Finance, Inequality and the Poor." *Journal of Economic Growth* 12 (1): 27–49. doi:10.1007/s10887-007–9010–6.

Becker, Gary, Kevin Murphy, and Robert Tamura. 1990. "Human Capital, Fertility, and Economic Growth." *Journal of Political Economy*.

Bedecarrats, F, J Bastiaensen, and F Doligez. 2012. "Co-Optation, Cooperation or Competition? Microfinance and the New Left in Bolivia, Ecuador and Nicaragua." *Third World Quarterly* 33 (1): 143–61. doi:10.1080/01436597.2012.627 245.

Behrman, Jere R., Susan W. Parker, and Petra E. Todd. 2010. "Do Conditional Cash Transfers for Schooling Generate Lasting Benefits? A Five-Year Followup of PROGRESA/Oportunidades." *Journal of Human Resources* 46 (1): 93–122.

Bertranou, Fabio, and Roxana Maurizio. 2012. "Semi-Conditional Cash Transfers in the Form of Family Allowances for Children and Adolescents in the Informal Economy in Argentina." *International Social Security Review* 65: 53–72.

Binswanger, H. 1980. "Attitudes toward Risk: Experimental Measurement in Rural India." *Journal of Agricultural Economics* 62: 395–407.

Bohn, Simone R. 2011. "Social Policy and Vote in Brazil: Bolsa Família and the Shifts in Lula's Electoral Base." *Latin American Research Review* 46 (1): 54–79. doi:10.1353/lar.2011.0003.

Brau, J., and G. Woller. 2004. "Microfinance: Review of the Existing Literature." *Journal of Entrepreneurial Finance and Business Venture* 1 SRC—G: 1–26.

Brau, James C., Shon Hiatt, and Warner Woodworth. 2009. "Evaluating Impacts of Microfinance Institutions Using Guatemalan Data." *Managerial Finance* 35 (12): 953–74. doi:10.1108/03074350911000025.

Bräutigam, Deborah A., and Stephen Knack. 2004. "Foreign Aid, Institutions, and Governance in Sub-Saharan Africa." *Economic Development and Cultural Change* 52 (2): 255–85.

Bresser-Pereira, Luiz Carlos. 2002. "Brazil's Quasi-Stagnation and the Growth Cum Foreign Savings Strategy." *International Journal of Political Economy* 32 (4): Taylor & Francis: 76–102.

———. 2009. *Developing Brazil: Overcoming the Failure of the Washington Consensus*. Boulder, CO: Lynne Rienner.

Bruha, Patrick. 2014. "Facts About Bolsa Família." *Brazil Business*, August 25. http://thebrazilbusiness.com/article/facts-about-bolsa-familia.

Bueno de Mesquita, Bruce, and Alastair Smith. 2011. *The Dictator's Handbook: Why Bad Behavior Is Almost Always Good Politics*. New York: PublicAffairs.

Burnett, John. 2010. "Drug War Forces Residents to Flee Mexican Town." National Public Radio, November 15.

Busse, Matthias, and Carsten Hefeker. 2007. "Political Risk, Institutions and Foreign Direct Investment." *European Journal of Political Economy* 23 (2): 397–415. doi:10.1016/j.ejpoleco.2006.02.003.

Campion, Anita, Rashmi Ekka, and Mark Wenner. 2010. *Interest Rates and Implications for Microfinance in Latin America and the Caribbean*. 177. IDB Working Paper Series.

Carmignani, Fabrizio. 2011. "The Making of Pro-Poor Growth." *Scottish Journal of Political Economy* 58 (5): 656–84. doi:10.1111/j.1467–9485.2011.00563.x.

Chaffee, Wilber Albert. 2015. "Brazil." In *Politics of Latin America: The Power Game*, edited by Harry Vanden and Gary Prevost, 5th ed., 381–408. New York: Oxford University Press.

Chang, Ha-Joon. 2012. *23 Things They Don't Tell You About Capitalism*. New York: Bloomsbury Press.

———. 2014. *Economics: The User's Guide*. London: Penguin Press.

Chauvet, Lisa, and Patrick Guillamont. 2004. "Aid and Growth Revisited: Policy, Economic Vulnerability, and Political Instability." In *Toward Pro-Poor Policies: Aid, Institutions, and Globalization*, edited by Bertil Tungodden, Nicholas Stern, and Ivar Kolstad, 95–110. New York: World Bank and Oxford University Press.

Chaves, Sidney Soares. 2011. "Diagnóstico E Desafios Do Microcrédito No Brasil." *Revista Desenbahia*, no. 15.

Chong, Alberto, Mark Gradstein, and Cecilia Calderon. 2009. "Can Foreign Aid Reduce Income Inequality and Poverty?" *Public Choice* 140 (1–2). Springer: 59–84.

Christen, Robert Peck, Steven Schonberger, and Richard Roseberg. 2004. "Struggling through the 'Growth Versus Best Practice' Tradeoff: The CrediAmigo Program of the Banco Do Nordeste, Brazil." In *Scaling Up Poverty Reduction: Case Studies in Microfinance*, 1–14. Washington, DC: Consultative Group to Assist the Poor.

Collier, P. 2007. *The Bottom Billion: Why the Poorest Countries Are Failing and What Can Be Done About It*. Oxford: Oxford University Press.

Collins, D., J. Morduch, S. Rutherford, and O. Ruthven. 2009. *Portfolios of the Poor: How the World's Poor Live on $2 a Day*. Princeton, NJ: Princeton University Press.

Copestake, James. 2007. "Mainstreaming Microfinance: Social Performance Management or Mission Drift?" *World Development* 35 (10). Elsevier: 1721–38.

Cukierman, A. 1980. "The Effects of Uncertainty on Investment Under Risk Neutrality with Endogenous Information." *Journal of Political Economy* 88: 462–75.

Cull, Robert, Asli Demirgüç-Kunt, and Jonathan Morduch. 2009. "Microfinance Meets the Market." *Journal of Economic Perspectives* 23 (1): 167–92. doi:10.1257/jep.23.1.167.

Cull, Robert, Asli Demirgüç-Kunt, and Jonathan Morduch. 2011. "Does Regulatory Supervision Curtail Microfinance Profitability and Outreach?" *World Development* 39 (6): 949–65. doi:10.1016/j.worlddev.2009.10.016.

D'Alva Kinzo, M., and J. Dunkerly. 2003. "Brazil since 1985: Economy, Polity and Society." *Institute of Latin American Studies, University of London*.

Darney, Blair G., Marcia R. Weaver, Sandra G. Sosa-Rubi, Dilys Walker, Edson Servan-Mori, Sarah Prager, and Emmanuela Gakidou. 2013. "The Oportunidades Conditional Cash Transfer Program: Effects on Pregnancy and Contraceptive Use among Young Rural Women in Mexico." *International Perspectives on Sexual and Reproductive Health* 39 (4): 205–14. doi:10.1363/3920513.

Daude, C., and E. Stein. 2007. "The Quality of Institutions and Foreign Direct Investment." *Economics and Politics* 19: 317–44.

Daude, Christian, and Ernesto Stein. 2007. "The Quality of Institutions and Foreign Direct Investment." *Economics and Politics* 19 (3): 317–44. doi:10.1111/j.1468-0343.2007.00318.x.

De Janvry, Alain, Frederico Finan, Elisabeth Sadoulet, and Renos Vakis. 2006. "Can Conditional Cash Transfer Programs Serve as Safety Nets in Keeping Children at School and from Working When Exposed to Shocks?" *Journal of Development Economics* 79 (2): 349–73. doi:10.1016/j.jdeveco.2006.01.013.

De Janvry, Alain, and Elisabeth Sadoulet. 2006. "Making Conditional Cash Transfer Programs More Efficient: Designing for Maximum Effect of the Conditionality." *World Bank Economic Review* 20 (1): 1–29. doi:10.1093/wber/lhj002.

De Los Rios, Jessica, and Carolina Trivelli. 2011. *Savings Mobilization in Conditional Cash Transfer Programs: Seeking Mid-Term Impacts.*

De Soto, Hernando. 2000. *The Mystery of Capital: Why Capitalism Triumphs in the West and Fails Everywhere Else.* New York: Basic Books.

Demirgüç-Kunt, R., and J. Morduch. 2011. "Does Regulatory Supervision Curtail Microfinance Profitability and Outreach?" *World Development* 39: 949–65.

Dowla, Asif, and Dipal Barua. 2006. *The Poor Always Pay Back: The Grameen II Story.* Bloomfield, CT: Kumarian Press.

Driver, C., K. Imai, P. Temple, and G. Urga. 2004. "The Effect of Uncertainty on Authorization: Homogenous vs Heterogeneous Estimators Empirical Economics." *Empirical Economics* 29 (4): 115–28.

Duflos, E., and K. Imboden. 2003. "The Role of Governments in Microfinance." *Consultative Group to Assist the Poor* 19 (Helping to Improve Donor Effectiveness in Microfinance).

Dulles, John W. F. 2014. *Vargas of Brazil: A Political Biography.* Austin: University of Texas Press.

Dupas, P., and J. Robinson. 2010. "Savings Constraints and Microenterprise Development: Evidence from a Field Experiment in Kenya." *International Policy Center Working Paper 111.*

Dutra, Bruno. 2014. "Agências de Fomento Oferecem Crédito Mais Barato Para MPMEs Nos Estados." *Brazil Econônomico*, August 27. http://brasileconomico.ig.com.br/negocios/pme/2014-08-27/agencias-de-fomento-oferecem-credito-mais-barato-para-mpmes-nos-estados.html.

Dutta, Nabamita, and Sanjukta Roy. 2011. "Foreign Direct Investment, Financial Development and Political Risks." *Journal of Developing Areas* 44 (2): 303–27.

Duvendack, Maren, Richard Palmer-Jones, James Copestake, Lee Hooper, Yoon Loke, and Nitya Rao. 2011. "What Is the Evidence of the Impact of Microfinance on the Well-Being of Poor People?" *EPPI-Centre* 1912 (August).

Easterly, William. 2001. *The Elusive Quest for Growth: Economists' Adventures and Misadventures in the Tropics.* Cambridge: MIT Press.

———. 2006. *The White Man's Burden: Why the West's Efforts to Aid the Rest Have Done So Much Ill and So Little Good.* New York: Penguin Press.

Einhorn, Bruce. 2013. "After Stingy Aid to Typhoon Victims, China Tries Damage Control." *Bloomberg Business*, November 20. http://www.bloomberg.com/bw/articles/2013-11-20/after-stingy-aid-to-typhoon-haiyan-victims-china-tries-damage-control.

El-Zoghbi, Mayada, Barbara Gahwiler, and Kate Lauer. 2011. *Cross-Border Funding of Microfinance*. 70. CGAP (Consultative Group to Assist the Poor).

Enders, Walter, and Gary A. Hoover. 2012. "The Nonlinear Relationship between Terrorism and Poverty." *American Economic Review* 102 (3): 267–72.

Epstein, Marc J., and Kristi Yuthas. 2010. "Microfinance in Cultures of Non-repayment." *Journal of Developmental Entrepreneurship* 15 (1): 35–54.

Farmer, Paul. 2013. "Rethinking Foreign Aid: Five Ways to Improve Development Assistance." *Foreign Affairs*, December.

Ferguson, Niall. 2009. *The Ascent of Money: A Financial History of the World*. London: Penguin Press.

Fernald, Lia C. H., Paul J. Gertler, and Lynnette M. Neufeld. 2008. "Role of Cash in Conditional Cash Transfer Programmes for Child Health, Growth, and Development: An Analysis of Mexico's Oportunidades." *Lancet* 371 (9615): 828–37. doi:10.1016/S0140–6736(08)60382–7.

Ferreira, F. H. G., Phillippe G. Leite, and Martin Ravallion. 2010. "Poverty Reduction without Economic Growth?: Explaining Brazil's Poverty Dynamics, 1985–2004." *Journal of Development Economics* 93 (1). Elsevier B.V.: 20–36. doi:10.1016/j.jdeveco.2009.06.001.

Field, Erica, and Rohini Pande. 2007. "Repayment Frequency and Default in Microfinance: Evidence from India." Institute for Financial Management and Research: Centre for Microfinance Working Paper Series 20.

Field, Erica, Rohini Pande, John Papp, and Jeanette Park. 2012. "Repayment Flexibility Can Reduce Financial Stress: A Randomized Control Trial with Microfinance Clients in India." *PLoS ONE* 7 (9).

Filmer, Deon, and Norbert Schady. 2011. "Does More Cash in Conditional Cash Transfer Programs Always Lead to Larger Impacts on School Attendance?" *Journal of Development Economics* 96 (1). Elsevier B.V.: 150–57. doi:10.1016/j.jdeveco.2010.05.006.

Finnemore, Martha, and Kathryn Sikkink. 1998. "Norm Dynamics International and Political Change." *International Organization* 52 (4): 887–917.

Fiszbein, Ariel, and Norbert Schady. 2009. *Conditional Cash Transfers: Reducing Present and Future Poverty*. Washington, DC: World Bank. doi:10.1001/jama.298.16.1900.

Foguel, Miguel Nathan, and Ricardo Paes De Barros. 2010. "The Effects of Conditional Cash Transfer Programmes on Adult Labour Supply: An Empirical Analysis Using a Time-Series-Cross-Section Sample of Brazilian Municipalities." *Estudos Economicos* 40 (2): 259–93.

Fortin, Jacey. 2013. "Trillion Dollar Theft: In Developing Countries, Staggering Losses Due to Corruption Exceed Incoming Aid, Report Says." *International Business Times*, December 27.

Fried, Brian J. 2012. "Distributive Politics and Conditional Cash Transfers: The Case of Brazil's Bolsa Família." *World Development* 40 (5): 1042–53. doi:10.1016/j.worlddev.2011.09.022.

Frieden, Jeffry A. 1987. "The Brazilian Borrowing Experience: From Miracle to Debacle and Back." *Latin American Research Review*. JSTOR, 95–131.

Frieden, Jeffry A., and Paul Kennedy. 2006. *Global Capitalism: Its Fall and Rise in the Twentieth Century*. New York: W. W. Norton.

Gähwiler, Barbara, and Alice Nègre. 2011. *Trends in Cross-Border Funding*. 68072. Washington, DC: World Bank.

Galema, Rients, Robert Lensink, and Laura Spierdijk. 2011. "International Diversification and Microfinance." *Journal of International Money and Finance* 30 (3): 507–15.

Galiani, Sebastian, and Ernesto Schargrodsky. 2010. "Property Rights for the Poor: Effects of Land Titling." *Journal of Public Economics* 94 (9). Elsevier: 700–729.

Getubig, M., D. Gibbons, J. Remenyi, and B. Quinones. 2000. "Financing a Revolution: An Overview of the Microfinance Challenge in Asia Pacific." In *Microfinance and Poverty Alleviation Case Studies from Asia and the Pacific*, edited by J. Remenyi and B. Quinones. London: Pinter.

Ghosh, Suman, and Eric Van Tassel. 2011. "Microfinance and Competition for External Funding." *Economics Letters* 112 (2). Elsevier B.V.: 168–70. doi:10.1016/j.econlet.2011.03.037.

———. 2013. "Funding Microfinance Under Asymmetric Information." *Journal of Development Economics* 101 (March): 8–15.

Gilpin, R. 1987. *The Political Economy of International Relations*. Princeton, NJ: Princeton University Press.

Girod, D. 2011. "Effective Foreign Aid Following Civil War: The Nonstrategic-Desperation Hypothesis." *American Journal of Political Science* 56: 188–201.

Glewwe, Paul, and Ana Lucia Kassouf. 2012. "The Impact of the Bolsa Escola/Familia Conditional Cash Transfer Program on Enrollment, Dropout Rates and Grade Promotion in Brazil." *Journal of Development Economics* 97 (2). Elsevier B.V.: 505–17. doi:10.1016/j.jdeveco.2011.05.008.

*Global Microscope on the Microfinance Business Environment*. 2012. New York: Economist Intelligence Unit.

Globerman, Steven, and Daniel Shapiro. 2002. "Global Foreign Direct Investment Flows: The Role of Governance Infrastructure." *World Development* 30 (11). Elsevier: 1899–1919.

Goldfajn, Ilan, and André Minella. 2007. "Capital Flows and Controls in Brazil: What Have We Learned?" In *Capital Controls and Capital Flows in Emerging Economies: Policies, Practices and Consequences*. Chicago: University of Chicago Press.

Gordon, Lincoln. 2001. *Brazil's Second Chance: En Route toward the First World*. Washington, DC: Brookings Institution Press.

Green, Alan. 2011. "Institutions Matter, but in Surprising Ways: New Evidence on Institutions in Africa." *Kyklos* 64 (1). Wiley Online Library: 87–105.

Gulyani, Sumila, and Debabrata Talukdar. 2010. "Inside Informality: The Links between Poverty, Microenterprises, and Living Conditions in Nairobi's Slums." *World Development* 38 (12). Elsevier: 1710–26.

Haggard, Stephan, Andrew MacIntyre, and Lydia Tiede. 2008. "The Rule of Law and Economic Development." *Annual Review of Political Science* 11. Annual Reviews: 205–34.

Haggard, Stephan, and Lydia Tiede. 2011. "The Rule of Law and Economic Growth: Where Are We?" *World Development* 39 (5). Elsevier Ltd: 673–85. doi:10.1016/j.worlddev.2010.10.007.

Hall, Anthony. 2006. "From Fome Zero to Bolsa Familia: Social Policies and Poverty Alleviation under Lula." *Journal of Latin American Studies* 38 (4): 689–709.

———. 2008. "Brazil's Bolsa Família: A Double-Edged Sword?" *Development and Change* 39 (5): 799–822. doi:10.1111/j.1467–7660.2008.00506.x.

Hall, Robert E, and Charles I. Jones. 1999. *Why Do Some Countries Produce so Much More Output per Worker than Others?* National Bureau of Economic Research.

Harrison, Glenn W., Thomas F. Rutherford, David G. Tarr, and Angelo Gurgel. 2004. "Trade Policy and Poverty Reduction in Brazil." *World Bank Economic Review* 18 (3): 289–317. doi:10.1093/wber/lhhO43.

Handa, Sudhanshu, and Benjamin Davis. 2006. "The Experience of Conditional Cash Transfers in Latin America and the Caribbean." *Development Policy Review* 24 (5): 513–36. doi:10.1111/j.1467–7679.2006.00345.x.

Hege, Gulli. 1998. *Microfinance and Poverty: Questioning the Conventional Wisdom*. New York: Inter-American Development Bank.

Heilbroner, R. 1953. *The Worldly Philosopher: The Lives, Times, and Ideas of the Great Economic Thinkers*. New York: Touchstone.

Heller, Lauren R., and Kayla D. Badding. 2012. "For Compassion or Money? The Factors Influencing the Funding of Micro Loans." *Journal of Socio-Economics* 41 (6). Elsevier Inc.: 831–35. doi:10.1016/j.socec.2012.08.005.

Hermes, Niels, and Robert Lensink. 2007. "The Empirics of Microfinance: What Do We Know?" *Economic Journal* 117 (517). Wiley Online Library: F1–10.

Hermes, Niels, Robert Lensink, and Aljar Meesters. 2008. "Outreach and Efficiency of Microfinance Institutions." *SSRN Electronic Journal*, 1–29. doi:10.2139/ssrn.1143925.

Heston, Alan, Robert Summers, and Bettina Aten. 2012. *Penn World Table Version 7.1*. Center for International Comparisons of Production, Income and Prices at the University of Pennsylvania.

Houtzager, Peter P. 2008. "The Silent Revolution in Anti-Poverty Programs: Minimum Income Guarantees in Brazil." *IDS Bulletin* 38 (6): 56–63.

Hubbard, G., and W. Duggan. 2009. *The Aid Trap: Hard Truths about Ending Poverty.* New York: Columbia Business School Publishing.

Hulme, David. 2000a. "Impact Assessment Methodologies for Microfinance: Theory, Experience and Better Practice." *World Development* 28 (1). Elsevier: 79–98.

———. 2000b. "Is Microdebt Good for Poor People? A Note on the Dark Side of Microfinance." *Small Enterprise Development* 11 (1): 26–28. doi:10.3362/0957–1329.2000.006.

Hulme, David, and Thankom Arun. 2011. "What's Wrong and Right with Microfinance." *Economics and Politics* 46 (48): 23–26.

Hunt, J., and S. Laszlo. 2012. "Is Bribery Really Regressive? Bribery's Costs, Benefits, and Mechanisms." *World Development* 40 (2): 355–72.

Imai, K., T. Arun, and S. Annim. 2010. "Microfinance and Household Poverty Reduction: New Evidence from India." *World Development* 38: 1760–74.

Imai, K., R. Gaiha, G. Thapa, and S. Annim. 2012. "Microfinance and Poverty: A Macro-Perspective." *World Development* 40 (8): 1675–89.

Imai, K., S. Katsushi, and Md. Shafiul Azam. 2012. "Does Microfinance Reduce Poverty in Bangladesh? New Evidence from Household Panel Data." *Journal of Development Studies* 48 (5): 633–53. doi:10.1080/00220388.2012.661853.

Islam, Nazrul. 2009. "Can Microfinance Reduce Economic Insecurity and Poverty? By How Much and How?" DESA Working Paper 82.

Jenq, Christina, Jessica Pan, and Walter Theseira. 2012. *What Do Donors Discriminate On? Evidence from Kiva.org.*

Karlan, D., and J. Zinman. 2009. "Expanding Microenterprise Credit Access: Randomized Supply Decisions to Estimate the Impacts in Manila." Department of Economics Yale University Working Paper No. 68.

Karlan, Dean, and Nathanael Goldberg. 2011. "Microfinance Evaluation Strategies. Notes on Methodology and Findings." In *The Handbook of Microfinance*, 17–58. Singapore: World Scientific Publishing.

Karlan, Dean, and Jonathan Zinman. 2010. "Expanding Credit Access: Using Randomized Supply Decisions to Estimate the Impacts." *Review of Financial Studies* 23 (1): 433–64. doi:10.1093/rfs/hhp092.

———. 2011. "Microcredit in Theory and Practice: Using Randomized Credit Scoring for Impact Evaluation." *Science* 332 (6035): 1278–84. doi:10.1126/science.1200138.

Kaufmann, Daniel. 2008. "Governance Matters VII: Aggregate and Individual Governance Indicators, 1996–2008" (June). World Bank Development Research Group Macroeconomics and Growth Team, Policy Research Working Paper 4978.

Khan, Sana. 2009. "Poverty Reduction Efforts: Does Microcredit Help?" *SAIS Review* 29 (2): 147–57. doi:10.1353/sais.0.0057.

Khandker, S. 1998. *Fighting Poverty with Microcredit: Experience in Bangladesh.* New York: Oxford University Press.

King, Elizabeth M., Stephan Klasen, and Maria Porter. 2009. "Women and Development." In *Global Crises, Global Solutions*, edited by Bjorn Lomborg, 2nd ed. New York: Cambridge University Press.

Kodama, Masahiro. 2012. "Aid Unpredictability and Economic Growth." *World Development* 40 (2). Elsevier Ltd: 266–72. doi:10.1016/j.worlddev.2011.07.015.

Kokko, Ari, Katarina Kotoglou, and Anna Krohwinkel-Karlsson. 2003. "The Implementation of FDI in Viet Nam: An Analysis of the Characteristics of Failed Projects." *Transnational Corporations* 12 (3). UN Transnational Corporations and Investment: 41–78.

Kolstad, I., and E. Villanger. 2008. "Foreign Direct Investment in the Caribbean." *Development Policy Review* 26: 79–89.

Krishna, A. 2010. *One Illness Away: Why People Become Poor and How They Escape Poverty.* Oxford: Oxford University Press.

Kumar, Anjali. 2005. *Access to Financial Services in Brazil.* Washington, DC: World Bank.

La Torre, Mario, and Gianfranco A. Vento. 2006. *Microfinance*. Basingstoke, UK: Palgrave Macmillan.

Lagarde, Mylene, Andy Haines, and Natasha Palmer. 2007. "Conditional Cash Transfers for Improving Uptake of Health Interventions in Low- and Middle-Income Countries: A Systematic Review." *JAMA* 298 (16): 1900–1910. doi:10.1001/jama.298.16.1900.

Lance, Justin Earl. 2014. "Conditional Cash Transfers and the Effect on Recent Murder Rates in Brazil and Mexico." *Latin American Politics and Society* 56 (1): 55–72. doi:10.1111/j.1548–2456.2014.00221.x.

Latifee, H. 2012. "The Future of Microfinance: Visioning the Who, What, When, Where, Why and How of Microfinance Expansion Over the Next 10 Years." *MicroCreditSummit.org* 10.

Levine, Robert M. 1998. *Father of the Poor?: Vargas and His Era*. Cambridge: Cambridge University Press.

Lewis, Neryl. 1999. "The Tasks of Political Recovery." In *Recovery from Armed Conflict in Developing Countries: An Economic and Political Analysis*, edited by Geoff Harris. New York: Routledge.

Li, Quan, and Adam Resnick. 2003. "Reversal of Fortunes: Democratic Institutions and Foreign Direct Investment Inflows to Developing Countries." *International Organization* 57 (01). Cambridge University Press: 175–211.

Limoeiro, Danilo. 2015. "Beyond Income Transfers: The Decline of Regional Inequality in Brazil during the 2000s." *Progress in Development Studies* 15 (1): 6–21.

Lomborg, Bjorn. 2014. *How to Spend $75 Billion to Make the World a Better Place*. Copenhagen Consensus Center.

Long, Scott. 1983. *Confirmatory Factor Analysis*. Beverly Hills, CA: Sage.

Louis, Philippe, Alex Seret, and Bart Baesens. 2013. "Financial Efficiency and Social Impact of Microfinance Institutions Using Self-Organizing Maps." *World Development* 46 (June). Elsevier Ltd: 197–210. doi:10.1016/j.worlddev.2013.02.006.

Ly, Pierre, and Geri Mason. 2012. "Competition between Microfinance NGOs: Evidence from Kiva." *World Development* 40 (3). Elsevier Ltd: 643–55. doi:10.1016/j.worlddev.2011.09.009.

Mahajan, Vijay. 2007. "Beyond Microfinance." In *Reducing Global Poverty: The Case for Asset Accumulation*, edited by Caroline Moser. Washington, DC: Brookings Institution Press.

Maisch, Felipe Portocarrero, Alvaro Tarazona Soria, and Glenn D. Westley. 2006. *How Should Microfinance Institutions Best Fund Themselves? Inter-American Development Bank*. Washington, DC: Inter-American Development Bank.

Mandelli, Misleine. 2013. "O Microcrédito Como Instrumento de Ascensão Socioeconômica No Sul Catarinense." Postgraduate paper, Universidade do Extremo Sul Catarinense.

Manor, James. 2007. *Aid That Works: Successful Development in Fragile States*. World Bank Publications.

Marconi, Reynaldo, and Paul Mosley. 2006. "Bolivia during the Global Crisis 1998–2004: Towards a 'Macroeconomics of Microfinance.'" *Journal of International Development* 18 (2): 237–61. doi:10.1002/jid.1218.

Marshall, M. G., K. Jaggers, and T. Gurr. 2012. *Polity IV Project: Political Regime Characteristics and Transitions, 1800–2010. Dataset User's Manual.*Vienna, VA: Center for Systemic Peace, 2011.

Martone, Celso. 2003. "The External Constraints on Economic Policy and Performance in Brazil." In *Brazil Since 1985: Politics, Economy and Society*, edited by Maria D'Alva Kinzo and James Dunkerly. London: Institute of Latin American Studies, University of London.

Maslow, A. 1943. "A Theory of Human Motivation." *Psychological Review* 50 (4): 370–96.

Mcintosh, Craig, Elisabeth Sadoulet, Steven Buck, and Tomas Rosada. 2013. "Reputation in a Public Goods Game: Taking the Design of Credit Bureaus to the Lab." *Journal of Economic Behavior and Organization* 95 (November): 270–85.

Meade, Teresa A. 2010. *A Brief History of Brazil.* Infobase Publishing.

Meagher, Patrick, Pilar Campos, Robert Peck Christen, Kate Druschel, Joselito Gallardo, and Sumantoro Martowijoyo. 2006. *Microfinance Regulation in Seven Countries: A Comparative Study.* IRIS Center, University of Maryland.

Medialdea, Bibiana. 2013. "Brazil: An Economy Caught in a Financial Trap (1993–2003)." *Revista de Economia Política* 33 (3). SciELO Brasil: 427–45.

Mersland, Roy, and Ludovic Urgeghe. 2013. "International Debt Financing and Performance of Microfinance Institutions." *Strategic Change* 22: 17–29. doi:10.1002/jsc.

Mezzera, Jaime. 2002. "Microcredit in Brazil: The Gap between Supply and Demand." *MicroBanking Bulletin*, November.

*Microfinance and Financial Inclusion: At a Glance.* 2014. World Bank. http://go.worldbank.org/XZS4R3M2S0.

Miller, Margaret. 2000. "Credit Reporting Systems around the Globe: The State of the Art in Public and Private Credit Registries." Presented at the Second Consumer Credit Reporting World Conference, held in San Francisco, California, October.

———. 2003. *Credit Reporting Systems and the International Economy.* Cambridge, MA: MIT Press.

Montgomery, Heather, and John Weiss. 2011. "Can Commercially-Oriented Microfinance Help Meet the Millennium Development Goals? Evidence from Pakistan." *World Development* 39 (1). Elsevier Ltd: 87–109. doi:10.1016/j.worlddev.2010.09.001.

Morduch, J. 2010. "Borrowing to Save: Perspective from Portfolios of the Poor." Financial Access Initiative.

Morgenthau, Hans. 1962. "A Political Theory of Foreign Aid." *American Political Science Review* 56 (2): 301–9. doi:10.2307/1952366.

Moser, Caroline. 2007. "Asset Accumulation Policy and Poverty Reduction." *Reducing Global Poverty: The Case for Asset Accumulation.* Washington, DC: Brookings Institution Press, 83–103.

Mosley, Paul. 2001. "Microfinance and Poverty in Bolivia." *Journal of Development Studies* 37 (4). Taylor & Francis: 101–32.

Moss, Todd W., Donald O. Neubaum, and Moriah Meyskens. 2014. "The Effect of Virtuous and Entrepreneurial Orientations on Microfinance Lending and Repayment: A Signaling Theory Perspective." *Entrepreneurship Theory and Practice* (May). doi:10.1111/etap.12110.

Most, B., and H. Starr. 1989. *Inquiry, Logic and International Politics*. Columbia: University of South Carolina Press.

Mota Lopes, Bruno, and Renato Macedo. 2012. "Microcrédito Na Bahia: Um (Des) Virtuoso Percurso Evolutivo." *Leituras de Economia Política* 13 (16).

Mukherjee, Joyita. 1997. "State Owned Development Banks in Microfinance." *Consultative Group to Assist the Poor, Focus Series* 10.

Murphy, K., A. Shleifer, and R. Vishny. 1991. "The Allocation of Talent: Implications for Growth." *Quarterly Journal of Economics* 106: 503–30.

Navajas, Sergio, Mark Schreiner, Richard L. Meyer, Claudio Gonzalez-Vega, and Jorge Rodriguez-Meza. 2000. "Microcredit and the Poorest of the Poor: Theory and Evidence from Bolivia." *World Development* 28 (2): 333–46. doi:10.1016/S0305-750X(99)00121-7.

Nichter, Simeon, Lara Goldmark, and Anita Fiori. 2002. *Understanding Microfinance in the Brazilian Context*. BNDES Microfinançe.

North, Douglass C. 1990. *Institutions, Institutional Change and Economic Performance*. Cambridge University Press.

North, Douglass, Daron Acemoglu, Francis Fukuyama, and Dani Rodrik. 2008. *Governance, Growth and Development Decision-Making*. Washington, DC: World Bank.

Novelli, José Marcos N, and Andréia Galvão. 2001. "The Political Economy of Neoliberalism in Brazil in the 1990s." *International Journal of Political Economy* 31 (4). Taylor & Francis: 3–52.

Odell, Kathleen. 2011. "Measuring the Impact of Microfinance Taking Another Look." Grameen Foundation Publication Series.

Olsen, Tricia D. 2010. "New Actors in Microfinance Lending: The Role of Regulation and Competition in Latin America." *Perspectives on Global Development and Technology* 9 (3): 500–519. doi:10.1163/156914910X499796.

O'Neill, Jim. 2012. "The Brazilian Miracle." *International Economy* 26 (1). International Economy Publications: 71–74.

Ostrom, Elinor. 1990. *Governing the Commons: The Evolution of Institutions for Collective Action*. Cambridge: Cambridge University Press.

Pachico, Elyssa. 2009. "'No Pago' Confronts Microfinance in Nicaragua." In North American Congress on Latin America, New York, October.

Pereira, Gilvanete Dantas de Oliveira. 2005. "Efeitos Do Microcrédito Sobre O Fortalecimento Dos Microempreendimentos E Sobre as Condições de Vida Dos Microempreendedores: Um Estudo Do Ceape; PB, No Período de 2001 a 2004." Universidade Federal da Paraíba.

Popkin, Samuel L. 1979. *The Rational Peasant: The Political Economy of Rural Society in Vietnam*. Los Angeles: University of California Press.

Porter, Michael. 1998. "Clusters and the New Economics of Competition." *Harvard Business Review* 76 (6): 77–90.

Rasella, Davide, Rosana Aquino, Carlos a T. Santos, Rômulo Paes-Sousa, and Mauricio L. Barreto. 2013. "Effect of a Conditional Cash Transfer Programme on Childhood Mortality: A Nationwide Analysis of Brazilian Municipalities." *Lancet* 382 (9886). Elsevier Ltd: 57–64. doi:10.1016/S0140–6736(13)60715–1.

Ravallion, Martin. 2009. *A Comparative Perspective on Poverty Reduction in Brazil, China and India.* Policy Research Working Paper 5080.

Rawlings, L. B., and Gloria Rubio. 2005. "Evaluating the Impact of Conditional Cash Transfer Programs." *World Bank Research Observer* 20 (1): 29–55. doi:10.1093/wbro/lki001.

Remenyi, J., and B. Quinones. 2000. "Is There a 'State of Art' in Microfinance?" In *Microfinance and Poverty Alleviation: Case Studies from Asia and the Pacific*, edited by J. Remenyi and B. Quinones. London: Pinter.

Rodrik, Dani, and Romain Wacziarg. 2005. "Do Democratic Transitions Produce Bad Economic Outcomes?" *American Economic Review*: 50–55.

———. 2008. "Second-Best Institutions." *American Economic Review* 98 (2): 100–104.

Roett, Riordan. 2011. *New Brazil.* Washington, DC: Brookings Institution Press.

Rohter, Larry. 2012. *Brazil on the Rise: The Story of a Country Transformed.* Macmillan.

Roodman, David. 2012. *Due Diligence: An Impertinent Inquiry into Microfinance.* Washington, DC: Center for Global Development.

Rosenberg, Richard. 2007. *CGAP Reflections on the Compartamos Initial Public Offering: A Case Study on Microfinance Interest Rates and Profits.* https://www.cgap.org/sites/default/files/CGAP-Focus-Note-CGAP-Reflections-on-the-Compartamos-Initial-Public-Offering-A-Case-Study-on-Microfinance-Interest-Rates-and-Profits-Jun-2007.pdf.

Roy, Sanjukta. 2011. "Foreign Direct Investment, Financial Development and Political Risks." *Journal of Developing Areas* 44 (2): 303–27. doi:10.1353/jda.0.0106.

Sachs, Jeffrey. 2005. *The End of Poverty: Economic Possibilities for Our Time.* New York: Penguin Press.

———. 2008. *The End of Poverty: Economic Possibilities for Our Time. European Journal of Dental Education: Official Journal of the Association for Dental Education in Europe.* Vol. 12 Suppl. 1. doi:10.1111/j.1600–0579.2007.00476.x.

Saavedra, Juan Esteban, and Sandra Garcia. 2013. *Educational Impacts and Cost-Effectiveness of Conditional Cash Transfer Programs in Developing Countries: A Meta-Analysis.* 2013–007. USCDornsife Center for Economic and Social Research. CESR Working Paper Series.

Sandberg, Johan. 2012. "Conditional Cash Transfers and Social Mobility: The Role of Asymmetric Structures and Segmentation Processes." *Development and Change* 43 (6): 1337–59. doi:10.1111/j.1467–7660.2012.01799.x.

Schicks, J. 2007. "Developmental Impact and Coexistence of Sustainable and Charitable Microfinance Institutions: Analysing Bancosol and Grameen Bank." *European Journal of Development Research* 19: 551–68.

Schmidt, O. 2010. "The Evolution of India's Microfinance Market—Just a Crack in the Glass Ceiling?," no. ii. http://mpra.ub.uni-muenchen.de/27142/.

Schonberger, Steven. 2001. "Microfinance Prospects in Brazil." World Bank (Sustainable Development Working Paper).

Segura-Ubiergo, Alex. 2012. *The Puzzle of Brazil's High Interest Rates.* International Monetary Fund.

Selcher, Wayne A. 1998. "The Politics of Decentralized Federalism, National Diversification, and Regionalism in Brazil." *Journal of Interamerican Studies and World Affairs* 40 (4). Wiley Online Library: 25–50.

Sen, A. 1999. *Development as Freedom. The New England Journal of Medicine* 341. New York: Random House.

———. 1999. "Democracy as a Universal Value." *Journal of Democracy* 10 (3). Johns Hopkins University Press: 3–17.

Shoji, Masahiro. 2010. "Does Contingent Repayment in Microfinance Help the Poor During Natural Disasters?" *Journal of Development Studies* 46 (2): 191–210.

Sinclair, Hugh. 2012. *Confessions of a Microfinance Heretic: How Microlending Lost Its Way and Betrayed the Poor.* San Francisco: Berrett-Koehler.

Skidmore, Thomas. 1967. *Politics in Brazil, 1930–1964: An Experiment in Democracy.* New York: Oxford University Press.

Skidmore, Thomas, Peter Smith, and James Green. 2014. *Modern Latin America.* 8th ed. New York: Oxford University Press.

Soares, Fabio Veras, Rafael Perez Ribas, and Rafael Guerreiro Osório. 2010. "Evaluating the Impact of Brazil's Bolsa Familia: Cash Transfer Programs in Comparative Perspective." *Latin American Research Review* 45 (2): 173–90.

Standing, Guy. 2008. "How Cash Transfers Promote the Case for Basic Income." *Basic Income Studies* 3 (1): 1–30.

Tchakoute Tchuigoua, Hubert. 2014. "Institutional Framework and Capital Structure of Microfinance Institutions." *Journal of Business Research* 67 (10). Elsevier Inc.: 2185–97. doi:10.1016/j.jbusres.2014.01.008.

Thapa, G. 2010. "Sustainability and Governance of Microfinance Institutions: Recent Experiences and Some Lessons for Southeast Asia." *Asian Journal of Agriculture and Development* 4: 17–37.

Thompson, Shelley. 2011. "80 Simple Rules: The Effective and Sustainable 2009 Rwandan Microfinance Regulations." *Syracuse Journal of International Law and Commerce* 38 (3/4): 415–43.

Todd, Jessica E., Paul Winters, and Guy Stecklov. 2010. "Evaluating the Impact of Conditional Cash Transfer Programs on Fertility: The Case of the Red de Protección Social in Nicaragua." *Journal of Population Economics* 25 (1): 267–90. doi:10.1007/s00148–010–0337–5.

Travieso-Diaz, Matias F. 1995. "Some Legal and Practical Issues in the Resolution of Cuban Nationals' Expropriation Claims Against Cuba." *University of Pennsylvania Journal of International Business Law* 16: 217.

Trebilcock, Michael, and Jing Leng. 2010. "The Role of Formal Contract Law." *Virginia Law Review* 92 (7): 1517–80.

Tsaliki, Liza, Christos Frangonikolopoulos, and Asteris Juliaras, eds. 2011. *Transnational Celebrity Activism in Global Politics: Changing the World?* Chicago: University of Chicago Press.

"US House Prices: Realty Check." 2014. *Economist.*

Vanden, Harry, and Gary Prevost. 2015. *The Politics of Latin America.* 5th ed. New York: Oxford University Press.

Vanroose, Annabel. 2010. "Differences in the Development of the Latin American Microfinance Market: Identifying Reasons." *Investment Management and Financial Innovations* 7 (3): 41–52.

Weeks, Gregory. 2015. *Understanding Latin American Politics.* Upper Saddle River, NJ: Pearson.

Wiesner, Sophie, and David Quien. 2010. *Can "Bad" Microfinance Practices Be the Consequence of Too Much Funding Chasing Too Few Microfinance Institutions?* ADA, 2.

Wilson, Kim. 2007. "The Moneylender's Dilemma." In *What's Wrong with Microfinance?*, edited by Thomas Dichter and Malcolm Harper, 97–108. Warwickshire, UK: Practical Action.

Wood, G. D., and I. A. Sharif. 1997. *Who Needs Credit?: Poverty and Finance in Bangladesh.* London: Zed Books.

Woodruff, Christopher. 2001. "Review of de Soto's *The Mystery of Capital.*" *Journal of Economic Literature* 39 (4): 1215–23.

Zimmerman, Jamie, and Yves Moury. 2009. *Savings-Linked Conditional Cash Transfers: A New Policy Approach to Global Poverty Reduction.* Washington, DC: New America Foundation.

Zucco, Cesar. 2008. "The President's 'New' Constituency: Lula and the Pragmatic Vote in Brazil's 2006 Presidential Elections." *Journal of Latin American Studies* 40 (1): 29–49.

———. 2013. "When Payouts Pay Off: Conditional Cash Transfers and Voting Behavior in Brazil 2002–10." *American Journal of Political Science* 57 (4). doi:10.1111/ajps.12026.

# Index

*Note:* Page numbers in italics indicate figures and tables.

157

# About the Author

**Brian Warby** is assistant professor of political science at the University of Northern Iowa. He received his bachelor's degree from Brigham Young University and his PhD from the University of South Carolina. His research primarily focuses on poverty alleviation and development, though he has secondary interests in trade and sanctions, as well as transnational crime.

CPSIA information can be obtained at www.ICGtesting.com
Printed in the USA
BVOW08*0035201215

429457BV00002B/3/P